Non-Lethal Weapons:
A Fatal Attraction?

About the Authors

Dr Nick Lewer was educated at the Universities of Dundee and Bradford. He is currently a Research Fellow in the Centre for Conflict Resolution at the University of Bradford. In addition to having organized and contributed papers to conferences and workshops in many different parts of the world, he is the author of a number of publications, including *Physicians and the Peace Movement: Prescriptions for Hope* (London: Frank Cass, 1992) and *Something Must Be Done: Towards an Ethical Framework for Humanitarian Intervention in International Social Conflict* (Bradford Peace Research Report, 1993). He is also an editor of *International Peacekeeping News*.

Dr Steven Schofield was educated at the Universities of Manchester and Bradford. For four years he was a research fellow in the Department of Science and Technology Policy at the University of Manchester and since 1992 has been co-director of the Project on Demilitarization, based in Leeds. A specialist in the field of arms conversion in the post-Cold War era, he is the author of a number of studies, including Bradford University's School of Peace Studies Research Reports, *Employment and Security: Alternatives to Trident* (1986) and (with Malcolm Dando and Michael Ridge) *Arms Conversion in the United Kingdom* (1992). He is the Editor of *Prodem Briefings*.

Non-Lethal Weapons: A Fatal Attraction?

Military Strategies and Technologies for 21st-Century Conflict

---

Nick Lewer and Steven Schofield

ZED BOOKS
London & New Jersey

Non-Lethal Weapons: A Fatal Attraction? was first published in 1997 by Zed Books Ltd, 7 Cynthia Street, London N1 9JF, UK, and 165 First Avenue, Atlantic Highlands, New Jersey 07716, USA.

Typeset in Monotype Baskerville by Lucy Morton, London SE12
Printed and bound in the United Kingdom
by Biddles Ltd, Guildford and King's Lynn

A catalogue record for this book is available from the British Library
US CIP data is available from the Library of Congress

ISBN 1 85649 485 3 (Hb)
ISBN 1 85649 486 1 (Pb)

Contents

List of Tables

Acknowledgements

Many thanks to friends and colleagues who freely gave their time and advice, but especially to Barbara Panvel, Simon Whitby, Malcolm Dando, David Isenberg, Steve Metz, Alan Roland-Price and Ruth Camm for sharing their own work and for their invaluable comments on our first draft. Also thanks to the 'Renew UN' Network and the Joseph Rowntree Charitable Trust for helping to fund this research project.

Glossary of Acronyms

ARDEC	Armament Research Development and Engineering Centre (US)
ARPA	Advanced Research Projects Agency (US)
ASEAN	Association of South-East Asian Nations
AWACS	Airborne Warning and Control Systems
BI	Benign Intervention
CN	'Tear Gas' (chloroacetophenone)
CS	'Tear Gas' (2-chlorobenzylidenemalononitrile)
CWC	Chemical Weapons Convention
DoD	Department of Defense (US)
DoE	Department of Energy (US)
EMP	Electro-Magnetic Pulse
ICBM	Intercontinental Ballistic Missile
ICRC	International Committee of the Red Cross
LCMS	Laser Countermeasure System
LEA	Law Enforcement Agency
LSD	Lysergic acid diethylamide
MIRV	Multiple Independent Re-entry Vehicles
MTR	Revolution in Military Technology
NATO	North Atlantic Treaty Organization
NGO	Non-Governmental Organization
NLW	Non-Lethal Weapon

NIJ	National Institute of Justice (US)
OAS	Organization of American States
OASDSOLIC	Office of the Assistant Secretary of Defense for Special Operations and Low Intensity Conflict
OAU	Organization of African Unity
OOTW	Operations Other Than War
OSCE	Organization on Security and Co-operation in Europe
OTA	Office of Technology Assessment
R&D	Research and Development
RMA	Revolution in Military Affairs
ROE	Rules of Engagement
RUC	Royal Ulster Constabulary
SAARC	South Asian Association for Regional Co-operation
UAV	Unmanned Aerial Vehicle
UNBIF	United Nations Benign Intervention Force
UNWC	United Nations 'Inhumane' Weapons Convention
USMC	United States Marine Corps

Introduction

The story of non-lethal weapons could be told as a mixture of science fiction, Orwellian dystopia and Strangelove paranoia – of Star Trek phaser guns set to stun rather than kill, global surveillance from spy satellites and mind-control drugs to command instant obedience. Tempting as it is to embrace these literary genres, our ambitions are more modest. In this book we will outline the historical background to the development of non-lethal weapons; make an initial analysis of non-lethal weapons and examine the debates surrounding their utility; look at the priorities for their research, development and deployment over the next five to ten years; describe doctrine and policy considerations; locate these weapons within the framework of existing weapons conventions and arms control treaties; describe past operational scenarios in which non-lethal weapons have been deployed; and conceptualize a future role for non-lethal weapons in peace enforcement and peacekeeping operations.

Much of the current available information comes from the USA where, during the early 1990s, increased interest was shown in non-lethal weapons, with an active and public debate involving government departments, military planners, academics and strategic analysts. Amidst much publicity, specially trained US marines were sent to Somalia in 1995 equipped with a variety of non-lethal weapons. At the same time the other US armed services were also investigating operational requirements. Research is under way in national and commercial laboratories on a range of technologies with non-lethal applications including lasers, electronics, biological and chemical agents, and acoustics. Although other countries are engaged in areas of non-lethal weapons research, the USA remains the most advanced in terms of the scale of research and the level of informed analysis.

Two major strands of argument have emerged. For some (but by no means all) in the armed forces and government, non-lethal weapons represent a potentially valuable addition to existing capabilities. For others, particularly amongst analysts in academia and think-tanks, they are at the heart of a revolutionary change in the nature of warfare. Military planners acknowledge that the world now is very different one from the world of the Cold War, with a range of growing threats such as terrorism; the proliferation of weapons of mass destruction; the breakdown of nation-states and ensuing risks to regional stability; the international dimension to drug operations and other major criminal activities. Broadly, the military response to these would be described as 'operations other than war'. Increasing demands have been made also on the United Nations to become involved in peace-keeping and peace enforcement actions.

Most people involved in these debates stress that the option of lethal force will remain. Crucially, conventional warfare continues to be the main priority for strategic planning. Therefore, non-lethal weapons are subordinate to a new generation of weapons which have increased lethality through greater accuracy and enhanced command and control. Even the term 'non-lethal' has caused considerable difficulty, with options such as 'disabling', 'less than lethal', 'strategic immobilizers', and even 'pre-lethal' having their supporters. However, we have retained the term 'non-lethal weapons' to stress the objective of keeping casualties to a minimum by not intentionally aiming to kill or seriously injure, particularly in the scenarios for peacekeeping.

Others argue that the diffuseness of new threats renders traditional force structures and priorities redundant. Without a radical refocusing around non-lethal weapons, the USA will be hopelessly unprepared to prevail in the variety of scenarios that will characterize twenty-first-century warfare.

While these perspectives on the operational utility of non-lethal weapons differ radically, they share a technological view of warfare that has its apotheosis in US military planning. Implicit in both camps is the assumption that the USA's advantage against any potential adversary rests on its lead in virtually all sectors of military technology. Indeed, a key feature of this book will be to place the debate about non-lethal weapons in the wider context of rapid technological change affecting all types of weaponry. Describing this as a revolution in military technology borders on a semantic exercise, because the imperative to maintain the technological edge demands a constant flow of innovations and added capabilities. However, the emphasis on command and control, information processing and smart weapons reflects the importance of the broader dynamic of change in electronics technologies affecting both the civil and the military sectors.

In other words, while many people have been shocked by the speed with which concepts of non-lethality have been absorbed into military planning and weapons development, the real surprise would have been if non-lethal weapons had not been developed in the USA. Perhaps they could be said to represent the ultimate attempt at military/technological solutions to a complex range of societal, as well as traditional military, conflicts.

Whilst research in the USA and other countries represents a major focus of discussion, the question of the deployment of non-lethal weapons with UN forces in peace support operations is an area receiving more attention. The deployment of such weapons in these scenarios raises ethical and humanitarian questions regarding the criteria and guidelines for their use, the long-term health and environmental impact, the danger of impinging on international arms control conventions, and the danger of lowering the threshold of intervention by the international community into the affairs of another state. But non-lethal weapons also offer a wider range of options to UN forces before they would have to resort to lethal force.

In writing such a book, it is always tempting to digress from these questions and to follow the more exotic pathways of non-lethal weapons development. Certainly, the question of the direction and secrecy that surrounds new weapons research always merits speculation on the ultimate use of such weapons. This could relate more, in the minds of conspiracy theorists, to the use of non-lethal weapons in social control than to 'legitimate' military and police uses. The evidence on previous generations of technologically advanced military systems suggests that what we do not know may well be more significant than what we do know. But the most important contribution this book can make at this juncture is to give the reader an appreciation of the issues facing us all in what could be a crucial period for the integration of non-lethal weapons into military strategies, into UN peacekeeping operations, and into civil law enforcement up to the end of the twentieth century.

Chapter 1 will define and categorize the main types of non-lethal weapons and place them within the broader contexts of a revolution in military affairs and the international political forces that are shaping both national and collective security requirements. Chapter 2 explores the main weapons programmes in the USA and the technological development of non-lethal weapons within these, and also looks at the issues that surround their research and development. Chapter 3 focuses on the policy and doctrinal development of thinking on non-lethal weapons, and looks at how they could be integrated into operational and tactical strategies. The experience of past uses of non-lethal weapons will be illustrated using cases from Northern Ireland, Vietnam, Somalia, and Iraq.

In Chapter 4 we will consider the legal and ethical aspects of the use of non-lethal weapons with respect to national and international laws and conventions, matters of conscience, and the dangers they pose to human life. Finally, in Chapter 5 we speculate on the use of non-lethal weapons as primary and integral parts of a conceptualized United Nations Benign Intervention Force and within a broad philosophy termed Benign Intervention. To do this we have to consider the argument that has historically raged around an independent UN military force, and questions concerning the politicization and militarization of humanitarian intervention.

1

Non-Lethal Weapons and
the Post-Cold War Environment

This introductory chapter serves to define non-lethal weapons and to place them in the context of broader issues, including the new international security environment at the end of the Cold War and changes to military strategy and doctrine. Recognizing that both controversy and uncertainty exist in the debate on the future of international relations, we simplify a very wide range of academic approaches into three 'world models' that allow us to speculate on the West's perception of threats and risks, and on the role of military force into the twenty-first century.

As an extension of this approach we look at the debate surrounding non-lethal weapons – contrasting those proponents who argue that they represent a useful capability in addition to conventional force with those of their supporters who elevate non-lethal weapons as a potentially radical breakthrough that requires fundamental changes in military strategy. Some initial evaluation is made of the concept of non-lethality, but specific analysis of non-lethal weapons' technologies and of operational issues will be the focus of subsequent chapters.

Definitions of Non-Lethal Weapons

Defining non-lethal weapons is no easy matter. The term 'non-lethal' has been subject to criticism as both a euphemism and an oxymoron when applied to weapons. Other terms have been suggested that are said to reflect more accurately the true nature of non-lethal weapons, including 'less-than-lethal', 'disabling', 'soft-kill', 'pre-lethal' and 'worse-than-lethal'.

Proponents of non-lethal weapons acknowledge that ambiguity exists since the use of any weapon brings with it the risk of injury and death. But they argue that the term 'non-lethal' accurately reflects the intention neither to kill nor to harm permanently. For this reason they reject the terms 'disabling' or 'less-than-lethal' because they imply permanent effects (such as loss of limbs). Opponents argue that more accurate descriptions would be either 'pre-lethal', implying temporary incapacitation in order to facilitate a follow-on attack with conventional weapons; or 'worse-than-lethal', to highlight the terrible psychological trauma that may affect individuals if the use of these weapons results in severe injuries – for example, blinding by lasers.

Certainly, the term 'non-lethal' has a reassuring connotation. Compared to lethal weapons, which have consistently killed and maimed not only troops but also civilians, the prospect of a new generation of weapons that could minimize injuries must resonate strongly with a popular opinion that has grown increasingly reluctant to countenance deaths and serious casualties through military action – especially in the era of instant media coverage. (Whether the other terms may, in fact, be more accurate will be the subject of detailed evaluation in Chapter 3.)

Three definitions of non-lethal weapons provide a useful introduction to the issues raised here. According to Kokoski, non-lethal weapons are

> those the purpose of which is detrimentally to affect either personnel or equipment with the result that they are less able to perform adequately the tasks to which they are assigned while at the same time minimising unintended collateral effects. (Kokoski, 1994, p. 369)

Similarly, a report for the Rand Corporation argues that non-lethal weapons are

> systems that can incapacitate an adversary's capability while attempting to prevent non-combatant injuries, friendly/adversary casualties and collateral damage. (Frost and Shipbaugh, 1994, p. 3)

In both cases the emphasis is on purpose and intent, with the caveat that no guarantee can ever be given of a casualty-free battle. Perhaps the most comprehensive definition in this context is provided by Christopher Lamb, Director of Policy and Planning in the Office of the Assistant Secretary of Defense for Special Operations and Low Intensity Conflict (OASDSOLIC).

> Non-lethal weapons are discriminate weapons that are explicitly designed and employed so as to incapacitate personnel or material, while minimising fatalities and undesired damage to property and environment. Unlike weapons that permanently destroy targets through blast, fragmentation, or presentation, non-lethal weapons have relatively reversible effects on targets and/or are able to discriminate between targets and non-targets in the weapon's area of impact. (Lamb, 1995, p. 1)

Here the focus is on the distinction between traditional, conventional weapons and non-lethal weapons. Of course, conventional weapons can be used in ways intended to harm temporarily rather than to kill but Lamb's emphasis on the types of effects caused by conventional weapons, which by their nature are longer-lasting, and the reversible effects of non-lethal weapons, remains an important one.

Before leaving the issue of definitions it is worth noting that some advocates of non-lethality suggest that there are qualitative differences between non-lethal weapons and conventional weapons that have profound implications for military operations and strategy (this issue is considered in detail below):

> Non-lethal weapons are weapons whose intent is to non-lethally overwhelm an enemy's lethal force by destroying the aggressive capability of his weapons and temporarily neutralizing his soldiers. (Morris, Morris and Baines, 1995, p. 24)

Even more ambitiously, perhaps, Alexander places them at the fulcrum of a revolutionary concept of warfare:

> Non-lethal defense concepts are comprehensive and far beyond adjuncts to present warfighting capabilities. Non-lethal defense has applicability across the continuum of conflict up to and including strategic paralysis of an adversary. (Alexander, quoted in Aftergood, 1995, p. 1)

Therefore, we have two major categories of definition, one that concentrates on the physical properties of weapons not intended to kill or permanently injure, and second that stresses their operational characteristics as a potentially radical break with traditional warfare.

Operational Categorization

Table 1.1 provides a list of the main weapons identified as non-lethal or potentially non-lethal. As can be seen, many different types of non-lethal weapons have been identified across widely disparate

Table 1.1 Types of non-lethal weapon

Type	Description	Operations	Target
Lasers			
High-energy	Destroy optical sensors	Vehicle- or aircraft-mounted	AM
Low-energy	Flash-blind people and disable optical sensors	Hand-held, vehicle- and aircraft-mounted	AM/AP
Pulsed-chemical	Produce high-pressure shock wave	Vehicle- or aircraft-mounted	AM
Optical munitions			
Uni-directional	Flash-blind	Artillery- or air-launched	AP
Isotropic	Flash-blind	Artillery- or air-launched	AP
Pulsing light	Disorientate	Vehicle-mounted	AP
Acoustic			
Infrasound beam	Disorientate	Vehicle-mounted	AP
	Disrupt material structures	Vehicle-mounted	AM
Bullet/pulse	Physical force weapon	Vehicle-mounted	AP
Microwave			
Repeat pulse	Disrupt electronic equipment	Vehicle and airborne	AM
Single pulse/EMP	Short-out power generation equipment, electronic equipment	Cruise missiles	AM
Chemicals			
Fuel/combustion modifiers	Degrade fuel in aircraft, tanks etc.	Direct deployment by military personnel	AM
Supercorrosives/supercaustics	Degrade materials	Direct/air-launched	AM
Embrittling	Degrade/crack materials	Direct/mortar/artillery	AM
Superadhesives Binding coatings	Produce rapid adhering of materials	Artillery/vehicle/aircraft	AM
Superlubricant anti-traction	Produce loss of traction		AM
Foams	Sticky and/or dense	Vehicle-mounted	AP
Calmatives/incapacitants	Affect human behaviour	Direct/vehicle-mounted?	AP

Type	Description	Operations	Target
Biological			
Biodeterioration	Degrade materials	Direct/vehicle-mounted	AM
Others			
Entanglers (nets, cables, chains etc.)	Trap vehicles/personnel	Direct/vehicle-mounted	AP/ AM
Conductive ribbons or wires	Short-out electrical systems and power-generation equipment	Cruise missile/ other guided missiles	AM
Conductive particles	Short-out electrical systems and power-generation equipment		AM/ ?AP
Stun weapons	Variety of hand-held electrical stunners	Direct	AP
Bullets	Wooden, rubber etc.	Direct/vehicle-mounted	AP
Computer virus	Alter or crash computer programs	Direct/network	AM
Disinformation/ deception	Political propaganda	Broadcasts/leaflets etc.	AP
Obscurants	Obscure sensors and vision (smoke-like substances)	Vehicle/aircraft	AP/ AM
Optical coating	Materials painted on optics or windows	Direct/small arms	AM

Note: AM: Anti-Material; AP: Anti-Personnel.

technologies. From an analytical perspective the multiplicity of weapons is confusing, and here we provide an initial categorization that groups weapons by shared characteristics, for example lasers, acoustics and so on, and concentrates on those identified in the recent literature.

We have included all the individual technologies in Table 1.1, but our major categories do not include electronic warfare (which already has wide-ranging applications) and psychological warfare (which does not seem appropriate in the context of the focus of categorization on clear and identifiable physical properties).[1] (For a detailed analysis of individual weapons, see Chapter 2.)

Main Technologies

Lasers

Lasers (light amplification by stimulated emission of radiation) are highly focused light sources (unlike ordinary light which radiates in all directions and at many different wavelengths) and with very wide power ranges: from one-hundredth of a watt to thousands of watts in continuous form, or through pulse power to millions of watts. Many applications exist, including industrial welding and cutting as well as new surgical procedures.

(i) *Anti-personnel*

In its anti-personnel form, a laser weapon would be aimed at the eye, causing dazzle or blindness. As the eye focuses the beam onto a small point on the retina, the brightness of the beam is effectively magnified by a factor of 100,000. Even low-powered laser rangefinders could be very damaging, and there are reports of serious eye damage, including the loss of a civilian's sight in Germany when a rangefinder was activated from a US tank. Moderate and high-power lasers directed at the eye would lead to severe eye damage including permanent blindness (International Committee of the Red Cross, 1993).

(ii) *Anti-equipment*

(a) Anti-sensor: In its anti-sensor role, the weapon works by scanning the enemy equipment with a low-power laser beam: if the beam enters the optical train of an enemy sensor system, a small fraction of light is reflected back. This locks the target and allows the weapon to increase the light, either overloading or damaging the enemy sensor.

(b) Anti-armour: It is also possible that pulsed chemical lasers could be used at very high power levels to cause a plasma blast wave affecting the properties of some materials; such a weapon could also have anti-personnel implications.

Optical munitions

(i) *Isotropic radiator*

Omni-directional radiators (ODRs) are broad-based visible light sources generated by the high-explosive shock of an inert gas that generates a very bright light as it is compressed. Isotropic radiators are not actually laser weapons but become incandescent at extremely high temperatures. They can be formed either as artillery shells or as air-launched bombs (Knoth, 1994).

(ii) *Directed radiator*

In constrast to the isotropic radiator, the directed radiator has a laser dye rod inside the munition to pump the light through the front of the shell in a single direction. This weapon has the advantage over low-energy lasers of utility in operations that are not dependent on line-of-sight firing (Knoth, 1994).

Microwaves

Electromagnetic wavelengths that bridge the frequency gap between normal radio waves and heat waves are known as microwaves. In their weapons form, high-powered microwaves operate by converting energy released from a conventional explosive into a radio-frequency energy.

(i) *Anti-equipment*

EMP (electro-magnetic pulse) is considered the most obvious military application. Conventional explosives can be carried in a small warhead such as a cruise missile to generate an EMP intended to overload sensitive electrical equipment, such as air defence electronics. Although no anti-personnel role has been identified, it is suggested that EMP may have effects on the brain, interfering with the neural networks and even causing unconsciousness (Fulghum, 1993b).

Acoustics

Human hearing covers wave frequencies between 20 and 20,000 cycles per second (or, between 20 and 20,000 Herz where 1 cycle per second is termed 1 Herz). Frequencies above this range are referred to as ultrasonics, whilst those below normal hearing are referred to as infrasonics. Infrasound, a tuned beam of low-frequency, high-intensity sound, can be generated by high-powered acoustic generators which set up vibrations that can affect both personnel and material (Picatinny Arsenal, NJ, 1992).

(i) *Anti-personnel*

Used as an anti-personnel weapon, an infrasound beam can resonate in certain body cavities causing disturbance of body organs, visual blurring and nausea. Effects can vary from temporary discomfort to permanent damage or death.

(ii) *Anti-material*

Possible effects against materials include embrittlement or fatigue of metals, thermal damage and delamination of composites. There is also the possibility of effects against buildings such as the shattering of windows, and even localized earthquakes.

Chemical and biological weapons

Chemical and biological weapons represent one of the most sensitive areas for non-lethal weapons. Chemical weapons already exist to alter human behaviour, and biological agents are being developed including organisms to degrade material in many weapon systems. Given the range of potential applications, it is useful to subdivide this category further.

(i) *Supercorrosives and supercaustics*

There is some confusion in the use of terminology to describe both corrosive and caustic chemicals, although the term 'supercaustic' seems to be used to cover both areas. Many chemical agents exist that are effective against equipment; for example, a mixture of hydrochloric acid (HCl) and nitric acid (HNO_3) can dissolve metals and organic compounds such as plastics, rubbers, polymers and glass.

(ii) *Liquid Metal Embrittlement (LME)*

There is some ambiguity in this area too, as LME can mean both metal embrittlement by means of a liquid and embrittlement by means of a liquid metal. The former would be a typical corrosive process by means of an acid. In addition, liquid metals like mercury can be absorbed causing a new material to be formed that is weaker or brittle. Operational difficulties exist with many of these chemical compounds, not least the need in many cases for direct application by a human agent.

(iii) *Combustion Alteration Technology*

Potential anti-material applications include chemical additives to change fuel, for example to increase its viscosity and turn fuel into gel, or the use of bacteria for similar ends (although this would be a slower process). Also in this category would be the use of particles to be ingested in the engine chamber, which would themselves burn so overheating the engine, and ceramic chaff used to destroy turbine blades.

(iv) *Anti-traction technology*

Anti-material applications would include the use of superlubricants to make surfaces slippery, or polymer adhesives that act as a superglue to freeze equipment. Such adhesives could be in a two-component form that sets after application, allowing aerial application.

(v) *Calmative agents*

Anti-personnel applications would include DMSO – dimethyl sulphoxide – a sedative which can be sprayed and is quickly absorbed through skin. Other agents include foul-smelling gases or aerosol sprays such as hydrogen sulphide (H_2S). A sticky foam has also been developed with the combined properties of chewing gum and shaving foam; this can spread on contact before sticking and immobilizing people. Similarly a bubble foam is now available that envelops people and can be laced with chemicals such as tear gas. This was deployed by US Marines in Somalia (see Chapter 3) (Knoth, 1994; International Committee of the Red Cross, 1994).

Others, including kinetic weapons

Many other proposed weapons exist that do not fall within this categorization, such as the use of sticky nets to trap fleeing vehicles, or electrified batons, but these tend to be at the lower end of the technological spectrum. Also, because the categorization in Table 1.1 focuses on the physical properties of weapons, it omits the controversial area of psychological warfare, including the interception and manipulation of an opponent's mass media. Many advocates of non-lethal weapons emphasize the role of disinformation, propaganda, etc., in special operations and this will be considered subsequently.

Analysis

Even a cursory analysis of non-lethal weapons provides serious grounds for concern. All the major weapons' technologies could, in certain circumstances, result in death or permanent incapacitation. Also, weapons designed for anti-material purposes could have anti-personnel effects, and in military operations it would be very difficult to ensure that only materials were damaged. Another obvious and significant criticism is that the development of some non-lethal weapons jeopardizes existing arms control agreements and conventions, undermining efforts by the international community to prevent weapons proliferation. Finally, international humanitarian law requires that weapons should not be indiscriminate or involve unnecessary suffering. Yet even where the intention is only to cause temporary incapacitation, much more severe and permanent injuries may result from the use of non-lethal weapons. (There are many examples in each of the categories and the following is simply intended to illustrate these problems. A full treatment of weapons technologies and operational issues is given in subsequent chapters.)

Hand-held lasers could be used either deliberately or inadvertently to blind people; the International Committee of the Red Cross is so concerned by the prospect of blinding lasers that recently it has led a very strong campaign to have them banned (see Chapter 4). Isotropic/flash weapons, particularly if used at night and when soldiers are wearing night-vision goggles which magnify available light, would almost certainly lead to permanent blinding.

Acoustic bullets can set up resonances in the body's cavities that could result not only in disorientation and nausea but in serious damage to the internal organs. Discriminating between mild and serious reactions will prove very difficult, especially as individuals may have very different reactions to the same intensity of sound wave.

It has been suggested that chemical agents such as supercaustics could be dispersed by aircraft as a spray. The implications for civilians caught under such an attack are obviously very serious. Similarly, superglues and adhesives could be employed directly against people or accidentally as a result of attempted application to immobilize equipment, causing severe skin damage. Superlubricants that are intended to interfere with logistical support by making runways, railways or roads too slippery to use would require widespread application. The impact might include dispersal by wind and rain over a wide area and into the water supply, with potentially long-lasting and serious environmental effects.

Moreover, the use of chemical agents for riot control is seen as a Trojan Horse to circumvent the Chemical Weapons Convention since the convention applies only to military uses. Similarly, the use of bacteria to destroy fuel supplies would directly contravene the Biological Weapons Convention, which forbids the development, production or stockpiling of biological weapons. Two of the major arms control agreements that emerged from the end of the Cold War are thus directly threatened by the introduction of non-lethal weapons (this is discussed further in Chapter 4).

But the momentum towards the deployment of non-lethal weapons is growing, and the reasons are to be found in the changing international security environment at the end of the Cold War.

International Relations into the Twenty-first Century

Before analysing the various approaches to the use of non-lethal weapons, it is important to place these approaches in the broader context of both military and strategic planning, as the end of the Cold War brought with it a renewed debate on the future of international relations. Given that the popular revolutions in Eastern Europe and the disintegration of the Soviet Union took almost everyone – not least academics – by surprise, it would be best to describe subsequent analysis as speculative rather than rigorously developed, but three main scenarios could be identified.

According to the first, the end of the Cold War signalled the emergence of a new, peaceful world order based on the model of Western capitalism. Derived very much from traditional liberal theory, this scenario saw military activity as undesirable and as a distraction from the main preoccupation of wealth creation within and between capitalist societies. Therefore, according to this scenario, a new and unprecedented opportunity now existed to develop a global consensus on the desirability of liberal democracy and the market economy that, in the longer term, would render conflict between nations an anachronism (Fukuyama, 1992).

Some use of military force might continue but would mainly be confined to small 'bushfires' such as Somalia and Cambodia – themselves a sad echo of the Cold War – while the vast majority of states would enjoy stability and prosperity. A massive peace dividend would be available for civil purposes, and the military would be relegated to a minor role.

In stark contrast to the liberal optimists, neo-realists see the 1990s as an inter-war rather than a post-war period. The collapse of the Soviet Union has led to the creation of a multipolar rather than a bipolar world in which the underlying rivalries between nation-states continue. Indeed, the potential for conflict has been increased by the emergence of new states in the former Soviet Union and elsewhere and by the growing economic and military power of countries in South-East Asia. Military conflict could even develop between current allies such as Japan and the USA because of intensifying economic competition.

Perhaps Huntington's analysis is the most comprehensive and certainly one of the most quoted, in which he describes 'fault-lines' in human society based on fundamental differences of culture and social structure that sustain long-lasting and unresolvable tensions:

> Non-Western civilizations will continue to attempt to acquire the wealth, technology, skills, machines and weapons that are part of being modern. They will also attempt to reconcile their modernity with their traditional culture and values. Their economic and military strength relative to the West will increase. Hence the West will increasingly have to accommodate these non-Western modern civilizations whose power approaches that of the West but whose values and interests differ significantly from those of the West. This will require the West to maintain the economic and military power necessary to protect its interest in relation to these civilizations. (Huntington, 1993, p. 49)

According to the neo-realists, the recent political changes, rather than leading towards the eradication of war and the release of resources for peaceful purposes, will have a reverse effect. Any cuts in military spending seen as a result of the end of the Cold War are a temporary phenomenon, and a reorientation of military capabilities will be required to face the new threats, with the emphasis on maintaining the West's technological advantage.

A hybrid of these two viewpoints characterizes a third approach. This holds that, effectively, there will be zones of peace and zones of turmoil, with economic and military co-operation between the advanced industrial societies in the zone of peace. However, the zone of turmoil will be by far the larger – including highly militarized states prepared to use force as well as states subject to intra-state conflict through civil war and religious fundamentalism (Singer and Wildavsky, 1993).

At its extreme this view postulates a future of resource competition, the breakdown of nation-states, and environmental degradation affecting billions of people at a time of rapid population growth outside the zone of peace. This has been described as the age of chaos:

> an epoch of timeless juxtapositions, in which the classificatory grid of nation-states is going to be replaced by a jagged-glass pattern of city-states, shanty-states, nebulous and anarchic regionalisms. (Kaplan, quoted in Miliband and Panitch, 1994)

According to the hybrid viewpoint, the West will need to maintain military capabilities against renegade states, or to apply intervention at the sub-national level should its interests be threatened directly or as a result of potential spill-over from localized conflicts. Here, any elements of liberal optimism on the benefits to Western societies through economic co-operation are subsumed under the implications for military planning. The West would need expanded operational capabilities across a broader spectrum than conventional warfare, in terms not simply of peacekeeping but also of special operations and covert warfare.

Of the three scenarios, the first was widely held in the early 1990s, especially with the fall of the Berlin wall and popular demands for a peace dividend. Certainly, the Clinton presidential campaign stressed the possibility of significant cuts in military spending and a programme to convert some arms productive capacity to other products, in order to enhance the USA's civil capabilities. A central argument was that the country's main security challenge in the twenty-first century would be its international economic competitiveness against not only Japan but also a unified European Community.

Such optimism was quickly replaced with concerns generated by the Gulf War and subsequently by the quagmire in the former Yugoslavia. The third scenario, therefore, seems most accurately to reflect events, at least in the short term, with co-operation between advanced industrial societies based on US military leadership against 'renegade states' or in situations of ethnic conflict and civil war. But Western military planners have not discounted traditional threats in the longer term, including a resurgent Russia or an aggressive form of Chinese nationalism, all of which serve to illustrate how fluid and uncertain the security environment remains.

The Revolution in Military Affairs

During the same period of uncertainty over international security issues, there have been rapid changes in military technology and operations that have led some commentators to describe this as a revolution in military affairs (RMA) and an associated military technology revolution (MTR). A more detailed analysis of the technological issues raised by non-lethal weapons will be made in Chapter 2. Here we concentrate on the major trends in weapons technologies and in military planning.

The armed forces have always looked to weapons innovation to maintain the technological edge deemed necessary for superiority or, ideally, supremacy in fighting wars. What is different, perhaps, in contemporary society is the rapid pace of change in civil technologies, and in particular electronics, which have profound implications for military operations. It is clear that in many fields of electronics technology, civil R&D is the technological leader and military applications of these essentially civil technologies appear widespread. But the time scales for evaluation and integration of new applications are notoriously longer in the military sector because of bureaucratic procedures, conservatism within the armed forces, and so on. The danger, from the military planning perspective, is that technology outstrips strategy and policy.

The goal of MTR has been described as battlespace control rather than any particular new, destructive weapons. Here, the emphasis is on the management and control of the battle with unprecedented levels of precision and speed. The main areas of concern, therefore, are information accumulation, command-and-control, and accuracy of weapons – all of which are dependent on innovations in various forms of electronics technology. Information can come in a variety of forms including via satellites, interception of enemy communications, field operatives and special forces. Command-and-control requires rapid integration of information and intelligence to speed up decision making while denying the same capabilities to the enemy through countermeasures such as electronic warfare equipment and anti-radar missiles.[2]

Great emphasis is placed on 'smart' weapons such as cruise missiles as the most effective way of translating the advantages gained through information accumulation and command-and-control into the ultimate objective of precision targeting. These weapons can, of course, be fired from traditional military platforms, allowing some continuity between new technologies and older systems, but the expectation is that the emphasis on smart weapons will grow.

The Gulf War and the Revolution in Military Technology

All these areas were highlighted during the Gulf War, which was said to prove the crucial importance of information gathering, speed of operations and accuracy of weapons. Information came from a variety of sources, including satellites, Airborne Warning and Control Systems

(AWACS) and ground commanders. Global positioning equipment enabled troop movements to be planned with unprecedented accuracy across very difficult desert terrain. Other sources of information included intelligence from covert operations behind Iraqi lines.

During the main battle, command-and-control provided real-time assessment of troop movements, helping to remove the 'fog of war'. And of course, as we saw on our television screens, advanced weapons, including cruise missiles using terrain mapping guidance systems and precision-guided munitions, were deployed extensively. Cruise missiles were even used in a non-lethal variant when, instead of carrying a conventional warhead, they were used to disperse carbon-fibre ribbons over power stations to short-out electrical power while retaining the capital equipment and buildings intact.

What tends to be ignored is the extent to which the USA relied mainly on traditional weapons for its Gulf War operations, including heavy bombs not dissimilar to Second World War munitions, and on fuel–air bombs. Even the use of cruise missiles for temporary disablement of power generation equipment was followed by destructive bombing of the buildings themselves. Nor has sufficient attention been given to problems with 'smart' weapons such as premature detonation and missed targets.

The popular perception that this was a 'surgical' war remains; according to this perception, aircraft and helicopter gunships using laser-guided munitions insulated the armed forces from direct combat, while increased accuracy concentrated force on military targets, and minimized civilian casualties.

To implement fully the Revolution in Military Affairs, however, requires fundamental change not only in technology but also in doctrine and organization. Despite the obvious superiority of Western forces in the Gulf War, many analysts believe that there still exists a yawning gap between that potential to maximize the use of new military technology and the constraints of traditional military planning. The jealously guarded autonomy of each of the armed services is reflected in their training and philosophies of warfare, coupled with a system of individual procurement budgets that institutionalizes separate weapons selection. Efforts are now under way in the USA to overcome some of these constraints, for example by co-ordination through the Joint Chiefs of Staff. But what is needed, according to one US strategist, is to integrate fully both doctrine and procurement, not only for traditional war fighting but for new requirements in the post-Cold War world:

in the years ahead the US military may operate in far more irregular than combined-arms environments and it therefore makes sense to build as much irregular capability into future weapons and forces as possible. This is especially true because if the MTR succeeds, potential adversaries, aware that they cannot win at the combined arms level, may resort to more insidious irregular operations to frustrate US aims. The goal will be to modify technologies, doctrines and force structures in ways that do not detract from their combined-arms-war-fighting and deterrent missions but that add greatly to their capabilities in irregular operations. A prominent example is special-operations which can perform a wide variety of missions in lesser-intensity warfare. (Mazarr, 1993, p. 10)

Future Roles for Non-Lethal Weapons

Here, the potential role of non-lethal weapons becomes clearer. Under a new range of operational requirements including conventional war, peacekeeping and special operations, the use of non-lethal weapons, according to their supporters, becomes not only desirable but, through improved technological capabilities, achievable.

For example, US Marines in Somalia deployed some of the new non-lethal weapons for the first time. The Marines were faced with potentially hostile crowds during the withdrawal of UN troops, and their gear included anti-riot equipment such as foam guns (dispersing a foam that could be laced with tear gas); sticky guns which ejected a material that set rapidly on impact to prevent movement; and various small rounds like wooden pellets and hard sponge which could knock people down while causing only temporary disablement and bruising (see Chapter 3).

The examples of anti-equipment cruise missiles in the Gulf War and anti-personnel weapons in Somalia reflect the spectrum from combined-operations/conventional warfare to lesser-intensity warfare including peacekeeping. Other anti-equipment weapons might include cruise missiles with EMP warheads to disable enemy command-and-control centres; lasers to blind optical equipment such as rangefinders; and caustic materials to damage military vehicles or tanks. As well as the anti-personnel equipment deployed in Somalia, acoustic, chemical and biological weapons could all be used to incapacitate people temporarily in similar peace enforcement situations (see Chapter 5).

Referring back to our original models, we can see that the neo-realist approach to international relations, with its emphasis on conventional force and deterrence, dominates military planning, albeit with some increased emphasis on other forms of conflict. Non-lethal weapons are now feasible within the broader framework of advances in military technology but are only a subsidiary element in military planning around conventional weapons systems.

The more radical perspective on non-lethal weapons suggests that the Military Technology Revolution and the new strategic environment require much greater emphasis on non-lethality as the basis for military doctrine and operations. In a world of chaos, the emphasis is on anarchy, the breakdown of nation-states, the spread of religious fundamentalism and other potentially violent social movements, all of which could be extremely damaging to Western interests and national security. Military strategy based on conventional war between nation-states is no longer a realistic basis for planning the use of force in these new conditions:

> Like a man who has been shot in the head but still manages to stagger forward a few paces, conventional warfare may be at its last gasp. As low-intensity conflict rises to dominate, much of what has passed for strategy during the last two centuries will be proven useless. The shift from conventional war to lower-intensity conflict will cause many of the most powerful and most advanced weapons to be consigned to the scrap-heap. Very likely it also will put an end to large-scale military-technology research and development as we understand it today. (van Creveld, 1991, p. 205)

The difficulty, of course, is to envisage realistic scenarios for the use of non-lethal weapons here in comparison to the existing or likely use of non-lethal weapons for peacekeeping or as part of conventional warfare. However, a common theme used to consider the feasibility of military operations dominated by the use of non-lethal weapons is the breakdown of law and order that threatens the stability of either a hostile or a friendly nation. For example, the collapse of communist rule in Cuba has been suggested as one possible scenario in which civil war might ensue and the West might intervene with the use of non-lethal weapons to support a pro-Western group (although the authors stress its use is to illustrate potential systems and technologies rather than to predict or endorse an actual intervention) (Metz and Kievit, 1994, pp. 25–7).

While not facing a direct military threat, the West would need to move rapidly in order to ensure a successful outcome. In this case, non-lethal weapons could be used against civil communications initially to paralyse telephone and computer systems. The West could then replace national broadcasting with its own propaganda for sympathetic political parties. Intelligence would already have identified and located hostile civil and military leaders, and a range of anti-personnel non-lethal weapons would be used to incapacitate these. One objective would be to identify individuals in large crowds and to target them in such a way as to avoid harming other civilians. Once a successful outcome had been achieved, the West could rapidly restore communications, power supplies, and so on, and provide financial and other aid to the new government.

The future of warfare, in these scenarios, becomes a complex interplay between civil and military operations, with no clear distinction between the two – hence the emphasis on psychological warfare and covert operations. Rarely stated but implicit in 'social warfare' is how non-lethality becomes the basis for permanent interference at the national and sub-national level whenever the West believes its interests are at stake.

In many ways, the distinction made above between the integration of non-lethal weapons into conventional warfare and their elevation as the basis of a new form of warfare is an artificial one when many crossovers exist, such as special operations. But the distinction is useful in clarifying how non-lethality produces different outcomes dependent on very different interpretations of military requirements. At this stage, we must emphasize that analysis of non-lethal weapons is still in its infancy and that most commentators seek to place them in the context of existing military strategy and doctrine.

Conclusion

It is clear that, far from sanitizing the battlefield, non-lethal weapons bring with them a whole array of potential dangers, including direct physical effects on people up to and including death or permanent disability such as blindness, as well as long-term environmental hazards. Serious questions are also raised about their impact on international treaties and conventions – such as the chemical and biological weapons conventions and on the inhumane weapons treaties – that attempt to ban weapons that cause unnecessary suffering.

Controversy exists over their operational utility, with many proponents arguing that the new international security environment at the end of the Cold War requires a fundamental re-evaluation of military strategy and doctrine in which non-lethal weapons can play a pivotal role. More commonly, non-lethal weapons are seen as a useful additional capability to conventional weapons in situations such as peace enforcement and special operations. Before we look at these operational issues in more detail, the next chapter focuses on weapons development, in order to establish exactly what priorities are emerging from the range of potential non-lethal weapons and what we can expect to see in the next five to ten years as deployed systems.

Notes

1. Many sources have been used in compiling this table. The main references are: Aftergood (1994); Cook, Fiely and McGowan (1995); Council for Foreign Relations (1995); Haseley (1992); Kanter and Brooks (eds) (1994); Victorian (1993).

2. Numerous sources exist on both the RMA and the MTR. The most useful for our purposes have been Aftergood (1995); *The Economist* (1995); Mazarr (1993); Metz and Kievet (1994; 1995).

2

Technology and the Invention of Non-Lethal Weapons

This chapter explores the technological development of non-lethal weapons. Using traditional weapons decision-making models from the Cold War era that stress the interaction of various organizations including weapons laboratories, military bureaucrats and the armed forces in determining choices and outcomes, we consider how non-lethal weapons fit into the general framework of weapons development. Particular emphasis is placed on the changing role of major weapons laboratories following the end of the Cold War as US federal policy reduced defence R&D while demanding greater commercial technological benefits from the remaining funding.

We will argue that this 'dual use' paradigm provides the major defence research institutions with a rationale for the maintenance of traditional areas of military work, including nuclear weapons, while extending their range of activities into conventional weapons research where these technologies have applications in the civil sector.[1] Non-lethal weapons fit comfortably into this framework, particularly directed-energy weapons such as lasers and acoustic weapons, which leads us to argue that the weapons laboratories have been one of the main types of institution promoting non-lethal weapons. However, secrecy poses serious barriers to a full understanding of the scale of research and the interrelationships between organizations.

Accepting that much work on non-lethal weapons is taking place under classified projects, we make an initial attempt to identify priorities for research, and to identify the progress of major weapons systems towards full development or production up to the end of the twentieth century. On the basis of this analysis we make a critical evaluation of existing 'catch-all' categorizations of non-lethal weapons that fail to clarify both substantial technological as well as operational differences between groups of non-lethal weapons, to the extent that even the term 'non-lethal' itself becomes problematic.

The Weapons Decision-making Process

At its simplest we can ask the question, where do non-lethal weapons come from? Are they the creation of scientists in the secret world of weapons laboratories; a response to demands from the military for new capabilities such as the growing emphasis on peacekeeping; the latest generation of hardware from defence contractors desperate for new sources of work since the end of the Cold War; or the brainchild of visionary strategists? In short, is there a technology push or a demand pull driving the search for new weapons?

Studies of the decision-making process around previous generations of weapons provide very different and conflicting interpretations of why particular choices of weapons are made. At one end of the spectrum it is argued that the role of the weapons laboratories and their scientists was pivotal. During the Cold War they produced a constant flow of weapons innovations that both the military and politicians were compelled to accept if they wanted to maintain the technological advantage against the Soviet Union.

Solly Zuckerman, the former Chief Scientific Adviser to the UK government, perhaps most vividly depicted this process during the height of the nuclear arms race:

> It is he, the technician, not the commander in the field, who is at the heart of the arms race, who starts the process of formulating a so-called military nuclear need. It is he who has succeeded over the years in equating, and so confusing, nuclear destructive power with military strength, as though the former were the single sufficient condition of military strength. The men in the nuclear weapons laboratories of both sides have succeeded in creating a world with an irrational foundation, on which a new set of political realities have to be built. They have become the alchemists of our time, working in secret ways which cannot be divulged, casting spells which embrace us all. (Zuckerman, 1980)

It would be easy, in the face of such powerful imagery, to generalize about an inevitable technological determinism driving the arms race. Various writers have made that case and Zuckerman's argument tends to be subsumed within it. However, his emphasis is on the role of the weapons scientists in their organizational setting, and the institutional power that they possess to influence decisively the direction of weapons R&D.

Other studies of the weapons decision-making process focus on bureaucratic and organizational models of the arms race that stress the roles of several bodies which include the military, the defence industries, government bureaucrats, politicians and the weapons scientists. Zuckerman's exclusive focus on the last ignores the inter-relationships between organizations, their alliances and conflicts, and shifts in the balance of power and influence. The importance of any one organization or group can and does vary, dependent on the case study under analysis.[2]

Even in the specific context of fundamental nuclear physics research that resulted in the development of the atomic and the hydrogen bombs in highly secret circumstances, and where the Zuckerman hypothesis would appear to have a strong superficial attraction, the historical record tells a very different story. The atom bomb, although advocated by scientists, most notably Einstein, was seen as a strategic necessity by politicians and military planners against the danger that Nazi Germany might develop nuclear weapons. Subsequently, the massive resources devoted to its development in the USA were subject to rigorous political and military control.

Nor was there much initial enthusiasm within the scientific community for the hydrogen bomb, despite the advocacy of some prominent scientists, such as Edward Teller. President Truman in fact surprised the scientific community when in January 1950 he announced advanced development work on the hydrogen bomb, since very little practical progress had been made. Scientific advisory groups were set up to deliberate on the advisability of an accelerated pro-gramme, and the majority were against such a course. Only the intervention of powerful advocates from the military and planning staff, against the background of heightened tension between the USA and USSR, tilted the balance in favour of those scientists advocating development (Blunden et al., 1989, pp. 88–96).

As the relationship between the superpowers deteriorated and the Cold War military establishment consolidated itself through the 1950s and 1960s, the monocausal view of weapons development becomes even more untenable. Many studies highlight complex bureaucratic processes and show that the military were often resistant to innova-tions, particularly if they threatened their core, strategic roles. For example, the US Air Force blocked research on ICBMs, probably the most potent symbol of the Cold War arms race, for several years in the early 1950s because they were seen to challenge the role of strategic bombers (Beard, 1976).

Similarly, in the 1960s, research on cruise missiles entered a crucial phase, with innovations in turbofan engines, designs of compact conventional and nuclear warheads, strong lightweight materials, and micro-electronics and map-making techniques for TERCOM (terrain contour matching). A strategic cruise missile was therefore a technical possibility, but the US Air Force again feared that the role of the bomber could be undermined and argued that cruise missiles should be limited to a short-range decoy role. Only political advocacy (based on budgetary concerns to provide cheaper and more effective strategic options to expensive bomber programmes) and support within the military bureaucracy of the Pentagon ensured that such opposition could be overcome. However, far from replacing traditional roles and force structures, cruise missiles were integrated into the US Air Force (and the navy) as additional capabilities (Graham, 1987).

The above examples draw on only a small part of the literature and do not give sufficient weight to the richness of interpretations that emerges from detailed studies of particular weapons, including the role of inter-service rivalries and of arms control agreements in stimulating as well as discouraging innovations (such as the MIRVing of missiles, that is, the development of multiple warheads, to overcome limits on missile numbers). The literature is focused on the USA and on nuclear weapons, partly because of the sheer magnitude of weapons research subjects afforded by the USA and the relative ease of access to research material. However, these examples do illustrate that even weapons that we now take for granted as symbols of a technological arms race are actually the product of contingent political and bureaucratic processes whose outcomes may not be clearcut and certainly cannot be analysed exclusively in technological terms. Supply-side models are an extremely useful analytical tool when they incorporate these complex interactions, but political factors and strategic demands need to be given proper consideration.

A New Technological Paradigm?

What does this tell us about the process of research and development on non-lethal weapons? Many of the organizations that one would expect to be active in researching and promoting non-lethal weapons in the USA are involved, but certain caveats need to be issued from the outset when making use of traditional bureaucratic models for analysis.

The overall context for weapons research has, of course, radically changed with the end of the Cold War. Total defence R&D has been cut, notwithstanding the massive lead that the USA enjoys, particularly since the collapse of R&D spending in the former Soviet Union. There are also intense pressures on a range of expensive weapons programmes. Most obviously, research on new generations of nuclear weapons appears to have been substantially cut (although simulations of explosions and stockpile management remain very important areas for the laboratories and recent evidence suggests that research on new forms of nuclear weapons is continuing).

Previous studies of the weapons research, development and acquisition processes took place in the context of stable conditions of superpower competition. In the new environment, there may be scope for a range of policy and research options. Therefore we need to look briefly at the overall policy for defence R&D and the rapidly changing nature of institutional structures and relationships before we can focus on the role of non-lethal weapons.

Even before the end of the Cold War there had been a fairly intensive domestic debate in the USA on the country's future as a global power in both military and industrial terms. Japan's clear leadership in what were seen to be strategic industrial sectors, the prospect of a stronger European Community under a single market, and the emergence of new high growth economies around the Pacific Rim all contributed to a mood of pessimism. This was reflected in a series of reports by academics and government agencies that advocated federal industrial and technology policies to give direct support to high-technology industries as the means of reversing relative economic decline. Paul Kennedy's best-selling book *The Rise and Fall of Great Powers* also touched a raw nerve by arguing that the USA suffered economically, as had other major military powers in the past, from the burden of large defence expenditures and global military commitments.

Broadly stated, these themes helped stimulate a climate in which the end of the Cold War was seen as an opportunity for the USA to refocus on economic rather than military challenges, and even to redefine international security on the basis of economic competitiveness. Arms conversion, with the federal government providing assistance to defence companies and to defence-dependent communities, was to be one important element of the transition to a post-Cold War economy.[3]

US federal R&D has been consistently important since the Second World War, albeit with some fluctuations. In 1992, the federal government spent $68.2 billion overall on R&D out of a national total of $157.4 billion. Of the federal share, $41.5 billion was defence-related. The nearest other category, health, was a distant second at 13 per cent of the federal R&D total, with civilian space and aeronautics, energy and general scientific research following behind. At times, defence R&D has been even more dominant – it reached a peak of 69 per cent of federal R&D in the mid-1980s but the Clinton administration is committed is to cut defence R&D to 50 per cent of total funding. It is estimated that defence R&D would decline to $25–27 billion (in constant 1992 prices) by the year 2001 if this ratio were to be achieved. But such projections need to be treated with caution since Republican opposition to defence reductions is strong, and defence R&D may well remain at existing levels in real terms into the twenty-first century.

The Department of Defense (DoD) has the biggest budget for its laboratories: $11.6 billion in 1992; this amount covers not only R&D laboratories but testing and evaluation centres. Less than half the DoD's total budget for laboratories is spent in-house; the rest is passed through to the private sector, mostly defence contractors. The Department of Energy (DoE) also has a significant role because of its responsibility for nuclear weapons research and development. It received $4.7 billion direct from the federal government in 1992, supplemented by about $1 billion from other departments, mainly the DoD. The main DoE weapons laboratories are Los Alamos and Lawrence Livermore, which design nuclear warheads, and Sandia, which engineers field-ready weapons using these warhead designs (OTA, 1993, pp. 12–17).

The Clinton administration's approach to technology and industrial policy is based on the concept of dual use – essentially the application of technologies to both the civil and the military sectors. Partly, dual use rests on the recognition that much of the driving force for technological innovation stems from the civil sector rather than the military, and that the economy in general should benefit from the federal budgets for research and development. All the weapons R&D institutions are required to improve their ratio of civil work as the administration attempts to break out of the traditional separation between the military and civil research/industrial bases. The ultimate objective would be to create a unified industrial base in which the federal programmes can meet military requirements while making a much greater contribution to a civil sector; the latter is itself seen as being of major strategic significance through international competitiveness (OTA, 1993, p. 18).

US Defence R&D Institutions

National laboratories

The DoE national laboratories faced the greatest challenge under the new dual-use policy, given their role as specialized nuclear weapons research centres. An intense debate developed over their ability to change, with many critics arguing that for obvious institutional reasons the laboratories are not best placed to carry out civil research. Traditionally, they have been mission-oriented for highly specialized defence requirements. R&D programmes have stretched over years if not decades, with the emphasis on performance rather than cost. Experience suggests that organizations find it very difficult to alter radically their traditional culture in the face of new demands and that the laboratories would be unable to adapt to the very different requirements of civil, commercial work.

In response, the laboratories have emphasized that their real expertise lies in core technological capabilities and not simply in the weapons developed through these capabilities. Perhaps most significantly, the laboratories have focused on their role in the chain of technological innovation, putting forward the case that their work can straddle basic research work carried out at universities and the near-market product development of industry, particularly as private sector R&D has declined in recent years. In other words, the laboratories see themselves as providing longer-term applied research that will be crucial to commercial competitiveness and for which neither universities nor private companies are best placed (Hecker, 1994; Narayanamurti and Arvizu, 1991).

The Clinton policy requires that 20 per cent of all funding should be focused on technologies that enhance US competitiveness, with a 'substantial' part of the remaining 80 per cent contributing to dual-use/dual-benefit activities. In response the laboratories have identified areas such as fusion energy, environmental clean-up technologies, and human genome mapping as some of their major capabilities that straddle defence and civil applications. From the perspective of US competitiveness, the laboratories argue that they are well placed to provide innovations that can assist the development of new industries in the longer term. However, efforts are also being made to increase commercial agreements with industry on specific applications of these core competencies that have more immediate industrial benefits. An example of this is Lawrence Livermore's contract with Boeing on polymer composites for the next generation of supersonic aircraft. (Lawrence Livermore National Laboratory, 1994, p. 5.) Defence work continues, but the laboratories have argued that much of their traditional nuclear work is now reoriented to the demands of dismantling nuclear weapons and to the monitoring of non-proliferation. Research in nuclear physics continues – the topics under investigation include laser fusion, flash x-ray machines and massive-parallel computer modelling of nuclear explosions, all of which could be applied to future nuclear weapons programmes. Conventional defence research, an area that previously constituted only a small proportion of the laboratories' work, is also being expanded; topics under investigation include sensors for submarine detection, multi-stage munitions, and new armour materials. (Lawrence Livermore National Laboratory, 1994, p. 21.)

Care should be taken in drawing general conclusions on the basis of these examples, given the laboratories' special characteristics as nuclear weapons research centres. But the laboratories' work does highlight several issues, including the different levels at which technology transfer is intended to operate: from long-term basic research to short-term commercial contracts with private industry. At the same time, nuclear and conventional weapons research continues, raising the question of how effective technology transfer to the civil sector can be if the emphasis remains on specialized weapons programmes.

ARPA – the Advanced Research Projects Agency

Formerly known as DARPA (it dropped 'defense' from its title under the general thrust of Clinton's technology policy), ARPA is a key organization for defence research and development in the USA. It is a separately organized agency in the Department of Defense with primary responsibility to maintain US technological superiority over potential adversaries. Particular emphasis is placed on managing and directing basic and applied research externally, rather than in-house, and on advanced technologies that can be applied across the armed forces in joint projects. In comparison with other research organizations, therefore, it is relatively small, but it is highly regarded because of both its emphasis on contracting out research and its relationship with the private sector. At a time of declining funding for the rest of the defence establishment, ARPA received increased funding, up from $1.4 billion in 1992 to $2.25 billion in 1993 (OTA, 1993, p. 28).[4]

With the federal government's increased emphasis on civil work, ARPA has been given responsibility for administering the Technology Reinvestment Programme. Bids are received from companies for research on new products or processes. These are evaluated on a competitive basis with both technological and commercial criteria emphasized. Companies are also required to provide matching funding if they are successful in winning ARPA support. Examples include pyrotechnic devices for vehicle rescue, and polymer composites for bridge reconstruction. Funding is modest and only provided to small and medium-sized companies; the larger defence companies have, through merger and takeover, consolidated around defence work. ARPA's mission remains predominantly defence-related, and the agency will not support any bid without a clear military application (ARPA, 1993).

Other Department of Defense laboratories

In 1993, the Army's Armament Research Development and Engineering Center (ARDEC) at Picatinny, New Jersey, employed over 4,500 people including 2,000 qualified scientists and engineers. It is the leading US laboratory for armaments, with responsibility for the management and procurement of initial production quantities and technical support. Current programmes include smart munitions (such as intelligent mines), tank artillery and advanced gun propulsion. Perhaps the latter is the most significant programme at present, with new facilities being built for electric guns and advanced composite railguns. The Army Research Laboratory at Adelphi, Maryland, employed 3,700 people in 1993 and covered the range of technologies and support for land warfare including information processing, battlefield environments, and vehicle propulsion (Department of Defense, 1994, pp. 2.6–2.9).

An overview

How far can dual use be considered a new technological paradigm, at least for federally supported R&D? There is no doubt that political support is strong, augmented by a range of programmes that provide real incentives to industry and research establishments. As far as industry is concerned, the major focus has been on small and medium-sized companies, whilst the prime contractors, responsible for a considerable level of military R&D, have in the main consolidated around specialized defence work.

The laboratories have stressed their core capabilities and new commercial orientations through licensing agreements with private industry. Work continues, however, on a range of specific military technologies with little or no civil and commercial benefit. Much of the dual-use research in the laboratories, particularly the emphasis on a long-term strategic role for the laboratories as centres of technological excellence that can provide path-breaking research in core areas that benefit both civil and defence sectors, seems little more than a convenient cover for business as usual.

This is the broader context in which research into non-lethal weapons is taking place. Already the laboratories have considerable expertise in technologies such as lasers and acoustics, which form the bedrock of much existing weapons development in this area. Given the continued emphasis on weapons research allied to the commercial application of core technologies, the laboratories are well placed to argue that their new mission provides an ideal framework for the development of non-lethal weapons. Indeed, the director of Los Alamos has cited non-lethal weapons as an area of expansion for the laboratories (Hecker, 1994, p. 49).

ARPA's emphasis seems to be on shorter-term research and commercialized technologies through the private sector. ARPA is also responsible for joint initiatives between the Department of Defense and the Department of Justice for specific non-lethal weapons programmes with the emphasis on affordability and applicability to both military and police roles.

DoD laboratories such as ARDEC play a key role in applying technologies more directly to specific military needs, and in working closely with industry. The private sector itself has its own research programmes, although development and production contracts are limited to a few areas. (See below for details.)

Institutional Support

Whilst the technological base for non-lethal weapons exists,[5] a strategic rationale was still lacking even into the early 1990s. In fact, many of the technologies that might form the basis of a non-lethal armoury had already been identified in the 1960s and 1970s but they were given no real priority in the context of Cold War military planning (SIPRI, 1978, pp. 202–9).

Only with the end of the Cold War and the re-evaluation of security issues was the potential of non-lethal weapons considered seriously. Compared to the 1970s, general technological advances had enhanced the prospects of developing fieldable equipment in terms of size, accuracy, speed of deployment etcetera. But, in themselves, technological advances would have been insufficient to secure funding without some strategic rationale that could attract support from influential organizations and individuals including government policy makers and the armed forces.

Two of the most active lobbyists have been Janet and Christopher Morris of the US Global Security Council, based in Washington DC. In a series of policy papers they provided a comprehensive analysis of what they termed the new 'age of chaos' and the role that non-lethal weapons might play in resolving conflicts in it. Significantly, the Global Security Council, whose chairman then was Ray Cline, the former deputy director of the CIA, had access to high-level government and military circles and seems to have been the catalyst for serious policy evaluation under the Bush administration.[6] But support at government level was far from unanimous, according to reports of these initial efforts. In the Pentagon during the early 1990s, Paul Wolfowitz, then Under Secretary of State for Policy and the director of a Non-Lethal Warfare study group, clashed with the Under Secretary of State for Acquisition, William Yockey, who opposed an expanded programme. Although some limited funding was agreed, even this was reportedly discontinued during the final two years of the Bush administration as the sceptics gained ascendancy (Hoshen et al., 1995).

By 1992, a new impetus to the development of non-lethal weapons emerged as the Clinton administration began a fundamental re-evaluation of defence priorities, culminating in the Bottom-Up Review carried out by the new Secretary of Defense Les Aspin. Policy papers were presented, in particular by John Alexander who was then director of the Los Alamos Disabling (Non-lethal) Technologies Program. With a background in military and special operations, Alexander stressed the potential that non-lethal weapons offered in the new strategic environment, with applications ranging from peacekeeping to full-scale conventional warfare, including 'strategic paralysis of an adversarial nation-state' (Alexander, quoted in Aftergood, 1995).

During 1993 and 1994, the first official endorsements of a research programme on non-lethal weapons were made. Emphasis was put on affordability and applicability. In other words this would not be an extravagantly funded programme like Star Wars, nor would it undermine the commitment to the funding of advanced technology for conventional war fighting. Where non-lethal weapons could make a contribution, as in operations like Somalia (see Chapter 3), and where they offered greater flexibility for the armed forces, they would be supported. A non-lethal weapons steering committee was set up, through the Office of the Under Secretary of Defense (USD) for Acquisition and Technology and the Office of the Assistant Secretary of Defense for Special Operations and Low Intensity Conflict (OASDSOLIC), with the remit to develop a 'master plan'. At the same time the US Department for Policy was given responsibility for strategic analysis while the US Department for Acquisition and Technology was expected to develop weapons programme options (Lamb, 1995, p. 2). Allied to these military/institutional developments was the significant growth of contacts with the civil sector, notably the Department of Justice (DoJ). In the aftermath of the Waco siege there were increasing demands for effective means of bringing such incidents to conclusion quickly and with minimum loss of life, including President Clinton's request for the development of non-chemical and non-lethal alternatives as riot-control agents.

A memorandum of understanding was signed between the Department of Defense and the Department of Justice in 1994 that led to a programme of research run by ARPA on technologies that could provide non-lethal applications for the DoD's Operations Other Than War and for the Department of Justice's civil security requirements, such as riot control, or the breaking of sieges.[7] Nor should we ignore the role that the armed forces played in non-lethal weapons development. Military commanders and the military police had all identified various operational requirements in which non-lethal alternatives might be useful. Requests for field testing of equipment were growing. For example the US Atlantic Command, responsible for deployments in Haiti, was actively considering the use of non-lethal weapons, and of course the US Marines deployed non-lethal equipment during the Somali evacuation (see Chapter 3).[8]

By the end of 1994, Charles Swett, Assistant for Strategic Assessment in the OASDSOLIC, had formulated a draft non-lethal weapons policy for discussion in early 1995 with the expectation that a final document would be agreed to form the basis for programmes to be incorporated into the 1996 defence budget and onwards for long-term procurement (Swett, 1994).

Compared to the situation in 1990–91, of major internal disagreement at the Pentagon and scepticism on the part of both politicians and many military planners, considerable support now existed and firm decisions were being taken, not only on specific weapons research but also on the integration of non-lethal weapons into defence planning. However, the issue of secrecy clouds any analysis of institutional support. Some of the leading advocates such as the Morrises argue that non-lethal weapons will achieve their greatest impact by means of an open assessment of capabilities and operational roles. Others, mainly from the traditional military establishments, argue that secrecy is of paramount importance to ensure maximum effectiveness. For example, there is the long-standing problem of proliferation once a technology is openly available and the need, therefore, to develop countermeasures. Many non-lethal weapons are based on the concept of impairing sophisticated electronic equipment, and it would be precisely countries like the USA that would be most vulnerable should an adversary have access to weapons of this kind.

At this stage, it would appear that the Clinton administration supports the traditional military perspective of secrecy on sensitive weapons programmes. If we do not know the full extent of research being carried out (and the growth of black programmes strongly indicates that some non-lethal weapons research is being kept secret), we can only speculate that other organizations, such as the CIA, may well have an input that influences the direction that non-lethal weapons are taking (Weiner, 1990).

Nor does an overarching policy statement from the DoD signify bureaucratic unanimity on non-lethal weapons. Research on electronic countermeasures and other forms of equipment-disruption weapons is well established. Similarly, psychological warfare has been supported for many years. Whether those institutions already active in such research would want their work subsumed under the broader heading of non-lethality remains to be seen, but we can expect considerable bureaucratic in-fighting if non-lethal weapons budgets begin to grow.

Non-Lethal Weapons Programmes

Having discussed the general questions of how non-lethal weapons fit into the institutional structures of weapons development, we can turn

Table 2.1   Main US weapons programmes

Type	Organizations	Stage of development
Lasers		
Hand-held Lasers	Lockheed/Sanders PLQ-5	Produced and deployed
	Army Communication Electronic Command	
Light-infantry lasers	Martin Marietta – Stingray	Produced and deployed
	ARPA	R&D
Pulsed chemical lasers	ARDEC/Los Alamos	R&D
Optical munitions		
Broad-beam isotropic	ARDEC/Los Alamos/Phillips	
Directed optical	ARDEC/Los Alamos	Tested (possibly deployed)
Acoustics		
Acoustic beam	SARA, ARDEC, Los Alamos	
Acoustic bullet	SARA, ARDEC, Los Alamos	Advanced development
HPM		
EMP (US Army)	ARDEC/Los Alamos/ Harry Diamond Laboratory	R&D
EMP (US Air Force)	Los Alamos/Eglin Air Force Base	Advanced development for Cruise AGM-86
Chemical and biological		
Foam and sticky materials	Sandia	Deployed
Anti-material compounds	ARDEC/CRDEC	R&D
	Los Alamos	R&D
Others		
Grenade-launched foam	ARDEC/Army Research Laboratory	Developed
Rubber bullet	ARDEC/Army Research Laboratory	Developed
Metal chaff	Los Alamos?	Deployed
Sticky nets, batons, strobe lights etc.	Various	Developed

to a more detailed analysis of specific programmes and funding. Using our existing categorization, Table 2.1 provides a summary of the main programmes.

Lasers

Lasers represent the most advanced of all non-lethal systems and possibly the most controversial. Research stretches back into the 1960s and lasers are now well established as rangefinders and as guidance systems for missiles and bombs. More recently – despite concerns that any battlefield use of laser weapons inevitably risks severe eye damage to personnel, up to and including blinding, and the concerted campaign, led by the International Red Cross, being waged to have lasers banned as inhumane weapons (see Chapters 1 and 4) – great efforts have been made to develop armour-mounted or hand-held laser weapons that can be used directly against equipment and personnel. The military stress the value of lasers for anti-equipment warfare, mainly through their ability to burn out sensitive optical elements.

As many as ten different laser programmes have been identified in the USA, the most important being the AN/PLQ-5 Laser Countermeasures Set (LCMS), manufactured by Lockheed/Sanders under a contract run by the Night Vision and Electronic Sensors Directorate of the US Army Communications–Electronic Command, Fort Belvoir, Virginia. LCMS is a portable laser mounted on a standard M-163A rifle. According to Lockheed, its primary role would be to detect, jam and suppress fire control, optical and electro-optical subsystems. Although the LCMS could be mounted on armoured fighting vehicles, the main emphasis has been on a portable version. Development and operational testing of the PLQ-5 in 1994 highlighted concerns over its weight; the US Army wants further development leading to a lighter weapon that could be hand-held rather than mounted on a rifle. An initial production contract of $80 million was awarded to Lockheed/Sanders in 1995 for 50 PLQ-5s with options for an additional 400 units to be used by light infantry and special forces (Hewish, 1995).

The US Army Communications–Electronic Command also instigated the Stinger Combat Protection System (AN/VLQ-7) developed by Martin Marietta as a heavier, vehicle-mounted laser; this was actually deployed during the Gulf War (although never actually used). The weapon first entered development in 1982 and a prototype was delivered to the US Army in 1986. As of 1995, Martin Marietta was completing work on a three-year Advanced Technology Demonstration (ATD) contract worth $68.4 million. Two other weapons deserve specific mention because of their different qualities as flash lasers. The Perseus 'optical flash' 40mm rifle grenade projectile was developed by the Los Alamos National Laboratory as part of its disabling technologies programme; its development was managed by the Armament Research, Development and Engineering Center (ARDEC). Perseus works by means of the light from an explosion, which pumps a laser bullet that emits a flash of white and laser light brilliant enough to blind both people and sensors temporarily.

Similarly, the Saber 203 grenade shell laser, developed by the US Air Force's Phillips Laboratory in Albuquerque, New Mexico, uses a grenade launcher to fire a high-brightness diode laser grenade. According to reports, Saber was deployed by the Marine Corps in Somalia but never used. More recently, Saber development has been taken over by the United States Special Operations Command and there is much speculation over how flash lasers would be deployed in the future. The US Air Force argues that glare and flash blinding 'can impair an adversary's ability to aim or reload a weapon ... drive a vehicle or leave the area' and that the system 'can also be useful to enforcement agencies for helping subdue or control criminals'.

Acoustic weapons

As yet, acoustic weapons have not received the attention given to lasers, but recent work is leading to the development of two new weapons. Both ARDEC and Los Alamos have been active in this area and a contract was placed in 1992 with Scientific Applications and Research Associates (SARA) of Huntingdon, California, to produce an acoustic beam and an acoustic bullet weapon. The acoustic beam is generated by a high-powered pulse which forces compressed air into an array of matched tubes to generate an infrasonic (low-frequency) wave front that can resonate causing damage up to and including 'localized' earthquakes. A high-frequency bullet would be emitted from a 1–2 metre antenna dish and this could effectively be set to different volumes to produce effects against personnel ranging from mild discomfort (such as nausea) to incapacitation and death (Starr, 1993, p. 320).

EMP weapons

Of the US national laboratories, Los Alamos has probably the highest profile, partly because of the advocacy work done by Alexander. It has also benefited from its long-standing relationship with the US

Air Force in the testing of EMP cruise missiles, a major focus of the laboratories' non-lethal weapons research. Reports of early work done in 1993 at Eglin air force base suggested that the main problem was focusing the electro-magnetic pulse on the target area in order to maximize damage to electronic systems. EMP research provides a useful example of dual-use technology as electro-magnetic pulses can be used for plasma physics research, high-pressure chemistry and fusion power. Explosives are added around the electronic coil in the cruise missile variant (Fulghum, 1993b, p. 61; Knoth, 1994, p. 37).

Chemical and biological weapons

Literally thousands of chemical and biological compounds exist that could be used for military purposes, but the main focus of attention seems to be on efforts to develop new supercorrosive and supercaustic agents. Los Alamos and ARDEC, along with other military laboratories, have investigated the potential of such agents to degrade military equipment but there are many problems, not least the potential hazards for personnel and the environmental impact. Most press attention has focused on sticky materials to inhibit movement, but again there are considerable question marks over the dangers should they come into contact with the eyes or cover the nose and mouth leading to breathing difficulties or even asphyxiation. At this stage, the only new chemical weapon actually deployed has been the foam gun which disperses an enveloping foam for use in riot control. Although the gun is not strictly a chemical weapon in itself, the foam can reportedly be laced with tear gas; deployment of the gas in this form is said to be more effective than the traditional grenade launching (Knoth, 1994).

Others

The literature on non-lethal weapons covers a range of other technologies, particularly those with both military and civil security applications. For example, many kinetic weapons are being investigated as an alternative to rubber bullets. Strobe lights are being considered as a means of disorienting and incapacitating crowds, whilst an array of sticky nets and other forms of entanglement is now being promoted to civil security forces.

Financial Support

Having looked at specific programmes, it remains to address the issue of financial support before making some tentative observations on the scale and maturity of non-lethal weapons' development.

As early as 1992, the US Army was reported to have $100 million available for non-lethal technologies, while the overall annual funds in 1994 had increased to an estimated $1 billion over the years 1994–97. The new program office for non-lethal weapons was allocated several new sources of funding under the 1996 appropriations including the transfer of funds from existing programmes, for example $17.8 million from the Tactical Technology (Advanced Land Systems) budget and $10 million from the Experimental Evaluation of Innovative Technologies budget. Significantly, the Armed Services Committee of the Senate noted the existence of other funds to support classified, non-lethal technology and recommended that a new Program Office for Non-Lethal Systems and Technology be given responsibility for co-ordinating all non-lethal programmes including classified ones (US Senate, 1995, pp. 108–9).

However, compared to the list itemized here, it has been suggested that the research laboratories alone have up to 24 different projects under way. Unfortunately, little information exists in the public domain on either their scale or their importance in the context of major development programmes. Nevertheless, such reports illustrate the difficulty of relying on public sources. Another complication is the allocation of funding. As we have seen, the categorization of non-lethal weapons is difficult, and some areas such as electronic warfare are excluded from funding as 'non-lethal weapons' in the USA for organizational reasons. The fact that much equipment, such as modular warheads on both cruise missiles and other 'smart' munitions, can be used for both lethal and non-lethal purposes begs the question of how research funds are allocated between conventional and non-lethal research programmes.

Priorities

We can see that an extensive range of research and development on non-lethal weapons is taking place in the USA. Interestingly, there seems to be a good level of co-operation between the laboratories and the armed forces research centres. The most significant work is taking place between ARDEC and both Los Alamos and Lawrence Livermore. In simple terms, ARDEC is concentrating on the development of delivery systems and munitions while the laboratories provide important support through their expertise in the basic sciences and applied physics. Similarly, the US Air Force uses the expertise in EMP research at Los Alamos to support the development of EMP cruise missiles.

ARPA seems quite separate from the other major research institutions but has an important role as supervisor of the joint Department of Defense and Department of Justice programme on Operations Other Than War/Law Enforcement, which includes non-lethal weapons. Research work is expected to be undertaken with the FBI through its facility at Quantico and the Special Entry Battle Laboratory of the Department of Defense's Special Operations Command. ARPA is also active in laser weapons research and has placed particular emphasis on rapid commercialization at low cost of a new generation of hand-held laser weapons.

Many other organizations are involved in non-lethal weapons research, especially in relation to small-scale police and security operations; they include the Department of Energy's National Engineering Laboratory with its Fleeing Vehicle Tagging Program, and the various programmes at the Law Enforcement Technology Center and at the National Institute of Justice.

By 1995, real advances had been made in lasers and isotropic weapons which had applications for all the armed services, and were already being deployed in small numbers. Acoustic weapons were nearing the production stage, with the main emphasis on army munitions although an air-mounted weapon was also considered feasible. While EMP research has experienced some difficulties, the potential effects have significant military value, if and when the problem of how to focus the direction sufficiently can be resolved. The extensive work on various chemical compounds such as supercorrosives can be expected to yield results in the next few years. Many small-scale research programmes, in the private sector and through the traditional small-arms and security sector, will also produce an array of low-technology non-lethal weapons, for example disablement of cars, tagging of fleeing vehicles, sticky foams, etc.

Of course, the problem of secrecy will always make this a partial and, to that extent, unsatisfactory projection of future priorities. But we feel that the areas emphasized here give a good indication of how, at least in the short to medium term, new non-lethal technologies may be incorporated into the armed services. Nor should we underestimate the rapid progress that can be made once a particular technological route has been identified. For example the US Air Force is reported to have made rapid improvements on the chaff dispenser first used in the Gulf War. A new version called the Wind Corrected Munitions Dispenser produces fibres so small, only a few thousandths of an inch, that they can degrade the performance of a whole range of military equipment, and with much greater accuracy compared to the initial dispenser technology (Rogers, 1995).

Non-Lethal Weapons and the Arms Trade

Although we have concentrated on the USA, there is also a broader, international context to non-lethal weapons R&D and a burgeoning trade in non-lethal weapons. Laser weapons provide the leading example, with many countries, including the UK, Russia and China, pursuing development. Since the early 1980s, the UK Royal Navy has deployed laser guns on warships to dazzle enemy aircraft pilots, while the Defence Research Agency was reported to have developed a tank laser system that has undergone extensive field testing. The former Soviet Union developed a variety of laser weapons, especially throughout its air defence network during the 1980s, and there is some evidence that lasers were used by Soviet forces in the Afghanistan war.

More recently, China has developed the ZM-87 Portable Laser Disturber, manufactured by China North Industries Corp (Norinco) and exhibited at an arms fair in South-East Asia in 1995. According to support documentation, the ZM-87 is designed not only to damage equipment but to dazzle and even blind the human eye at ranges of up to 3km.[8]

Information on other non-lethal weapons is very difficult to obtain, although there is evidence of considerable efforts in the former Soviet Union on psychological warfare and chemical/biological weapons. It would be no surprise if other countries with major defence R&D capabilities were carrying out at least preliminary work. For example, the UK government has recently undertaken a major evaluation of national research priorities through the Office of Science and Technology. Non-lethal weapons were endorsed as an area for expansion because of the probable increase in demand for UK troops in peacekeeping and peace enforcement operations.[9] Yet there is virtually nothing in the public domain on the extent of UK non-lethal weapons research, or on priorities for funding.

Despite a lack of concrete information we can make the general observation that, based on traditional patterns of weapons development, non-lethal weapons will become increasingly available through the arms trade. China's marketing of a laser weapon illustrates how rapidly that trade is developing and how it need not depend on equipment from the prime defence exporters, the USA, Russia, UK and France.

Second-tier suppliers like China are emerging as major competitors to the leading exporters, not only challenging them in their traditional markets but aggressively pursuing new customers around the Pacific Rim and the military dictatorships of the Third World. Intense competition in the context of oversupply and economic pressures on defence companies to raise their share in export markets to compensate for reductions in domestic procurement expenditure raises very serious issues about proliferation. Compared to many high-technology, conventional systems, non-lethal weapons can be marketed as relatively cheap alternatives and may even be sold at discounted prices in order to win new customers. Concerns have also been raised that terrorists may obtain non-lethal weapons. A laser attack on civilians is one of the disturbing scenarios being suggested now that hand-held lasers and the technology required for their assembly are readily available.

Such problems are not exclusive to non-lethal weapons, as the arms trade continues to raise issues of secrecy and accountability despite the recent efforts to set up a UN arms trade register. It is fair to say that the international community has yet to deal effectively with the impact of new weapons development on arms control and arms trade conventions. The recent efforts to have blinding lasers banned under the UN Inhumane Weapons Convention, while the trade in such weapons continues to grow, illustrates the difficulties in this area.

Conclusion

On the face of it, the end of the Cold War and uncertainties over future security requirements have created a very dynamic and fluid situation for decisions on new weapons. The USA's national defence laboratories, under pressure to justify continued federal support, stressed their core capabilities in basic and applied research which could be directed to civil innovations that made a contribution to national economic competitiveness. Overall reductions in defence R&D spending by the Clinton administration, and the emphasis on dual use in remaining funding, suggested a considerable swing from specialized defence research.

But defence R&D continues at a relatively high level and the research laboratories have consolidated around nuclear weapons research, new conventional weapons research and some efforts at commercialization of technology. Work on non-lethal weapons is attractive to the laboratories because it builds on their undoubted expertise in key technological areas such as lasers, while the potential civil use of these technologies can also be emphasized. It is not surprising, therefore, that the laboratories have been the main institutions behind the growth of work on certain types of non-lethal weapon. Certainly, at a time when the traditional model of defence R&D support is under threat, non-lethal weapons provide a useful element in the argument for continued R&D support.

Throughout the early 1990s non-lethal weapons were of growing importance to military planners, although R&D and the formulation of doctrine and strategy were for some time uncoordinated and haphazard. There was also inter-service rivalry for funding and resources associated with non-lethal weapons development. By the mid-1990s, however, although tensions still existed within and between political, research and military interests, R&D and the acquisition and deployment of non-lethal weapons became more organized and systematized. In March 1996 the US DoD proposed that the Commandant of the Marine Corps (USMC) be named as executive agent for non-lethal weapons to co-ordinate activities for all the armed services and the Special Operations Command within a Joint Non-Lethal Weapons Integrated Product Team (Starr, 1996). This team would also co-ordinate with other government agencies, such as the Department of Justice, and be under the overall direction of the Under Secretary of Defense responsible for acquisition and technology.

The growth of funding, albeit from low levels, and political and military endorsements strongly indicate that non-lethal weapons are now at the crucial stage of being firmly embedded into the broader framework of institutional support necessary for the introduction of a major new weapons programme.

But we are still left with some serious problems, including ones of definition and secrecy. Based on our initial categorization, any number of potential weapons – ranging from high-technology lasers and EMP cruise missiles to low-technology wooden batons – fall under the banner of non-lethal weapons. Our analysis indicates that US government-funded R&D has concentrated on a range of directed-energy programmes including laser, acoustic and EMP weapons. Federal government support for private-industry R&D has also been important; laser weapons are now being manufactured by defence companies and acoustic weapons are at an advanced stage of production.

High-technology research needs to be distinguished from other forms of non-lethal technologies such as those financed through ARPA's joint defence and civil security programme and from dual-use programmes that might result in weapons at the lower end of the technology spectrum. We can expect to see the private sector, including defence companies and security equipment manufacturers, develop many types of low-technology hybrid weapons for both military and civil security requirements.

On the issue of secrecy, we can only stress that much work is taking place on classified projects. Extrapolating from the priorities identified through public sources, it would be unsurprising if directed-energy and other high-technology weapons were the main focus, but which institutions are carrying out and supporting specific programmes and for what purposes (such as Special Operations) can only be a matter of speculation. There seems little doubt that the key emphasis in federal R&D support is on high-technology non-lethal weapons. From the traditional military perspective, these forms of weapons are consistent with the goal of superiority over any potential adversary by maintaining the technological superiority in conventional warfare. Below that, and with very different technological capabilities and requirements, come a range of less sophisticated technological programmes that straddle operations other than war, peacekeeping and civil security.

Compared to other multi-technology, multi-weapons programmes like Star Wars, this is a fundamental distinction. Despite the unattainability of its main objective to build an impenetrable anti-ballistic missile system, Star Wars had clear criteria around a range of high-technology, not to say exotic, weapons systems. These fed major R&D programmes in the laboratories and private industry.

A catch-all definition of non-lethal weapons lacks this mission focus and serves only to cloud rather than clarify major issues such as technological priorities and the integration of high-technology, non-lethal weapons into conventional war fighting. Suffice to say that an EMP weapon that disables enemy communications before a full-scale conventional attack and a sticky foam that stops a rioter from throwing a brick may both be called non-lethal weapons, but represent fundamentally different concepts of weapons research and operational criteria. This, in turn, has far-reaching implications for our analysis of non-lethal weapons, but we need to look in more detail at operational issues before we can give a comprehensive re-evaluation of non-lethality.

Notes

1. Here 'dual use' is used as a technological term as distinct from the main use elsewhere in the book which focuses on joint military and civil operations.

2. See, for example, Beard (1976); Graham (1987); Reiss (1992).

3. See for example, Renner (1992); and Markusen and Yudken (1992).

4. At the time of writing it appears that ARPA is planning to change its name back to DARPA again.

5. See, for example, Egner et al. (1977).

6. See Chapter 3 for a detailed analysis of operational issues.

7. 'DoD and DoJ Developing Technologies to Fight Similar Battles', *Defense Daily*, 23 March 1994.

8. N. Cook, 'Chinese laser "blinder" weapon for export', *Jane's Defence Weekly*, 27 May 1995.

9. Office of Science and Technology (1995), p. 195.

3

Policy, Doctrine, Strategy, Operations

This chapter will examine doctrinal, operational and tactical requirements of army and police forces, and look at how non-lethal weapons could be integrated into their operational strategies. Non-lethal weapons will not replace lethal weapons but be used in conjunction (or, ideally, where possible as a first choice) with them. Non-lethal weapons have operational applications across a broad spectrum of conflict scenarios from 'traditional' war fighting and civil control to the roles of peacekeeping and peace enforcement. The latter are partly defined by the needs of the United Nations and regional security organizations.

Spectrum of Conflict
PEACE → Civil disturbance → Conflict other than war → WAR

The components of this spectrum, which cover a wide range of activities, may be present in a situation in some combination, all at once, or only one element at a particular time. For example, regions in conflict often experience phases of peace; of localized terror, when different ethnic groups attack and slaughter each other; of terrorist attacks on civilian and military targets; of guerrilla or insurgent activity; and of general war. Military responses to particular components and phases of these components of the spectrum are often constrained by political considerations, both national and international in scale. There is also a demand from police forces for new technology to help them with managing and resolving situations such as sieges (for example, Waco) and hostage taking. Non-lethal weapons could have a use in the phase of conflict dynamics when talks have failed and there is a threat of all-out war. This use of non-lethal weapons before starting a 'conventional' war 'provides something new in global affairs – an intermediate phenomenon, a pausing place, an arena for contest in which more outcomes could be decided bloodlessly' (Toffler and Toffler, 1993, p. 134). These military and police forces and functions can be broadly categorized as follows:

1. State military forces: counter-drugs operations; against weapons of mass destruction; crowd control; battlefield operations (disabling personnel and softening up targets before use of deadly force) and operations other than war (OOTW); counter-terrorist actions; low-intensity warfare and special forces operations; protection of withdrawing forces; non-combatant evacuation operations (NEOs); conflict short of war; limits of usage (having to revisit targets); denial of service capabilities; escorting humanitarian aid convoys.
2. Insurgent/rebel forces: as for (1).
3. Paramilitary and civilian police forces: riot control; hostage situations; VIP protection; arresting and controlling violent criminals.
4. UN and regional economic and security organizations: peacekeeping and peace enforcement; escorting humanitarian aid; restoration of law and order; disaster relief.

A fifth category can be added:

5. Criminal and terrorist organizations: includes international drug cartels, piracy at sea, banditry, domestic criminal gangs, political and religious groups. Non-lethal weapons can, like any other weapons, be used in criminal and terrorist activities. Some involved in these activities have training in and access to advanced and developed technology bases. There is also a prolific international arms trade which is available to terrorists and criminals.

Military Perspectives

Military forces hope to incorporate non-lethal weapons technology into 'new age soldiering' within the context of developments such as the Soldier Modernization Plan (Tillman, 1994). Advisory, study and policy groups in the US and NATO have been focusing on doctrine, training, material and technical co-ordination in the research and development of new weapons systems, including non-lethal weapons. In 1994 a NATO study group was set up to undertake a reassessment of military doctrine as well as a rethinking of overall military planning and strategy. NATO laid down five main functional enhancements sought for the modern soldier: improved lethality, command-and-control, survivability, sustainment, and mobility. Military planners and politicians also have to take into account new non-aggressive roles for combat troops, such as peacekeeping, and the public's increasing unwillingness to accept casualties (Hewish and Pengelley, 1994). The emergence of the global media and the 'CNN factor' – the 'live' broadcasting of war fighting worldwide as it takes place – now heavily influences how a war is fought. Because of the public's faith in and expectation that new weapons technologies mean fewer casualties, politicians and soldiers are aware that positive and friendly domestic and world opinion is a vital factor in fighting a war, and any means that limit casualties on all sides are examined. But military commanders are also aware of the need to maintain a 'warrior culture' within the armed forces. The more 'police actions' the military are involved in, the more the public will want to see them accountable to civil law (civil rights and so on), and whilst non-lethal weapons give commanders more politically acceptable responses in violent situations, military leaders stress the fact that essentially their forces are still required to be prepared and trained for war fighting. This means that they need troops trained and equipped to win battles quickly, with as few casualties to their own troops as possible. Are assault combat troops the right elements to be used in situations where non-lethality is a prime concern? In war fighting, non-lethal weapons have a vital function in (1) command-and-control warfare which would include psychological operations, electronic warfare, military deception, operational security, information warfare, and the physical destruction of command-and-control capabilities (Barry et al., 1994, p. 7) and (2) as pre-lethal weapons to stop or hinder enemy systems, thus enabling a lethal strike.

Before we look more closely at factors influencing military policy on non-lethal weapons, and military doctrine, strategy and operational requirements, some clarification of this terminology is appropriate. There are myriad definitions in the literature for these terms, but we will use them within the following broad parameters:

- *Policy* – the course or general plan of action adopted by a government or party or person.

- *Doctrine* – constitutes fundamental guidance and direction and makes up the fundamental principles by which military forces or elements guide their actions in support of national and international objectives (a principle being the basic truth or a general law or doctrine that is used as a basis of reasoning or a guide to action or behaviour).
- *Strategy* – the planning and directing of the whole operation of a campaign of war.
- *Operation* – strategic military activities in war or during manoeuvres.
- *Tactics* – the art and science of the detailed direction and control of movement or manoeuvre of forces in battle to achieve an aim or task. Hence, a tactical weapon is used at close quarters, while a strategic weapon can reach enemy territory.

These terms, within the framework of non-lethal weapons, will now be explored in more detail.

Policy

Policy issues surrounding the research, development and use of non-lethal weapons are related to multiple factors which are influenced by concerns about both local and global interests at national level (sovereign states) and international level (collective security and humanitarian crises). There is often tension between the policy goals of the two levels relating to factors such as clashes of strategic national interests, differences of cultural and ethnic values, disagreements about appropriate responses to humanitarian crises caused by violent conflict or abuses of human rights, allegiances to international power or influence blocs, and economic and developmental considerations. The national and international policy requirements would coincide, for example, when UN Security Council members agreed on the need to intervene, with UN forces, in a humanitarian crisis.

Two main sets of factors that influence or shape non-lethal weapon military policy, doctrine, strategy and operational elements have been identified (Swett, 1994). These are domestic political factors, and global strategic factors. Domestic political factors include the fact that there is usually some political opposition to every proposed military action, that in the US for example there is public scepticism of the necessity for US military intervention overseas (particularly when (perceived) important American interests are not at stake), that there is an intolerance for civilian suffering, and that because of significant escalatory potential in all forms of intervention there is sensitivity in the US executive and legislative branches to the possibility of making a commitment and then having to back away from it, thereby damaging the USA's international credibility. Amongst important global strategic factors, Swett draws attention to the pressure for the USA to maintain regional stability in some areas through a military presence; the growth of regional economic, political and military organizations transcending national boundaries; the growth of regional organized crime syndicates and linkages to form international criminal organizations; the increasing political and economic refugee flows and illegal immigration which may be exacerbated by 'low-intensity conflicts'; continued major humanitarian problems; the accelerating erosion of government authority in some parts of both the developing and the developed worlds, causing states' inability to control their own territory, military and police forces, and the collapse of legal and administrative systems; and the continuing proliferation of weapons of mass destruction, especially into the hands of irresponsible regimes and terrorist groups.

Swett also formulates some general principles concerning US policy on non-lethal weapons. He points out that the USA needs additional options for the projection of its military power short of lethal force; that non-lethal weapons can make available significant new capabilities; that non-lethal weapons can be employed across the spectrum of conflict; that in certain situations overwhelming lethal military force is still necessary; that non-lethal weapons can inadvertantly cause fatalities; that any non-lethal weapon system should be consistent with international law and the principles of proportionality and discrimination; that non-lethal weapons will not replace/supplant other systems or cause a major shift in war fighting, or consume disproportionate resources; and that priority should be given to non-lethal weapons showing significant promise of dual use by law enforcement agencies (LEAs) as well as by the military. Governments should also consider the broader policy issues around non-lethal weapons. For example, how prominent a role should non-lethal weapons play in a defence posture: should it be high-profile, to maximize deterrence, or low-key, so as not to encourage development/proliferation of countermeasures? What kinds of non-lethal weapons should defence departments acquire and what kinds should not be acquired, for reasons like scarce resources, mission importance, legal obligations? Relating to legal and treaty obligations, do non-lethal weapons using hallucinogens or other psychotropic substances qualify as toxic chemicals or riot control agents under the Chemical Weapons Convention? In what circumstances should non-lethal weapons be used? And, given a choice, would it be preferable to kill a combatant or take actions that could leave him or her alive but permanently maimed?

A policy for acquiring non-lethal weapons should relate closely to their potential use as instruments in promoting national policy. For the USA Lamb states that the highest priority should be placed on developing and acquiring systems to support the following tasks, which he listed in descending order of importance (Lamb, 1994):[1]

- neutralize combatants intermingled with non-combatants;
- control crowds;
- disable or disrupt military logistics;
- disable or disrupt elements of, or the entirety of, a regional civil/ military communication, transportation, and energy infrastructure;
- disable or destroy weapons or weapon development/production processes, including suspected weapons of mass destruction.

Non-lethal weapons that show a significant promise of dual use by law-enforcement agencies as well as by the military services will receive higher priority than those that do not. Lamb's guidelines also state that only those non-lethal weapon programmes that satisfy the general requirements of technical feasibility, operational utility, and policy acceptability would be considered for support. Non-lethal weapons should satisfy the following criteria:

- they should contribute to the accomplishment of a task or tasks that may be assigned to US military forces;
- they should be considered with established US policies including arms control agreements or other international legal commitments that the USA is committed to observe;
- they should be technologically and operationally feasible;
- they should be affordable;
- they should have an acceptably low probability of being fatal or inflicting permanent disablement on personnel, and causing undesired damage to property and the environment;
- they should not be easily defeatable by enemy countermeasures once known; or if they could, the benefits of a single opportunity to use them in a given context would be so great as to outweigh that disadvantage;
- they should be able to achieve an effect that is worth the cost of the intelligence support they require.

Criticism of non-lethal weapons comes from all directions of the political spectrum. Lamb identifies objections from the 'left' as: non-lethal weapons will make war more likely by reducing its destructive consequences; they will violate international treaties and that some are unethical and inhumane; they will damage the environment; non-lethal weapons cost too much and/or don't work; and non-lethal weapon development is part of a military–industrial conspiracy to preserve influence in the post-Cold War world. From the 'right' of the political spectrum, non-lethal weapons come under attack because they indicate a real lack of military resolve; they encourage micro-management of the military by politicians; they weaken the effectiveness of US military forces; they put the lives of US soldiers at risk; and they do not produce the physical effects necessary to punish aggressors.

By August 1995 US Pentagon officials had almost completed their non-lethal weapon policy, research and acquisition plans (Capaccio, 1995b). Swett restated that 'we are not forcing a major shift in the way wars will be fought. We never will have non-lethal weapons standing alone. They will always be augmented, if necessary with lethal force.' The argument for non-lethal weapons was given a boost in a report from the influential Council for Foreign Relations (1995).[2] This came to the conclusion that non-lethal technologies have the potential for providing new strength for diplomacy, new credibility for deterrence, new flexibility for the military, and new strategic options for policy makers. The report also noted:

> Non-lethal options are, however, not a panacea, and require careful management of their potential and perils. At present, communications warfare, other non-lethal weapons options, and economic sanctions analysis are assigned to separate areas of the Department of Defense and other government agencies. Moreover, laboratory generated technological advances largely drive policy analysis, rather than national policy requirements shaping research. Given the long lead times historically associated with the adoption of innovations in military doctrine and training, the subject of non-lethal technology needs thorough analysis now. A national policy on non-lethal options should come from the National Security Council (NSC), in view of the varied and complex problems presented and the necessity to integrate military, economic, diplomatic, and political strategy. (Council for Foreign Relations, 1995, p. xii)

The debate that revolved around whether blinding lasers should be deployed engaged the policy question of the trade-off between the loss of international and domestic support for the armed forces, and an increase in effectiveness that would result from the US use of battle-field blinding and other maiming weapons.[3] Some analysts think that the banning of such weapons by major powers like the USA would mean that fewer were made, and those that were would be easier to keep track of. There was also the controversy that deployment of non-lethal weapons would contravene the Geneva Conventions and the UN Inhumane Weapons Convention (see Chapter 4).

In the 1990s other countries, including the UK, Germany and France, were formulating policy on non-lethal weapons. NATO looked at non-lethal weapons through its Defence Research Group and the Advisory Group for Aerospace Research and Development (AGARD). The AGARD report identified the goal of non-lethal air defence (NOLAD) as protecting territorial airspace with minimal harm and collateral damage. This could be achieved through three phases: warning, shock, and degradation, each graduating in intensity. Tech-nologies to enable this include anti-electronic measures, anti-structure chemical agents, and canopy masking polymer agents (Parent, 1995). The report added that specific and accurate delivery systems would have to be developed so that 'enemy' air crew would be convinced that these were effective capabilities. The AGARD report notes that NOLAD technologies have immediate application in the enforcement of no-fly zones in peace support operations (PSOs):

> These operations, which involve a high degree of political complication outside the military sphere, may benefit from the application of nonlethal measures against aircraft violating prescribed airspace. (quoted in Parent, 1995).

Doctrine

When policy has been articulated relating to the use of non-lethal weapons, then doctrine can be developed. Some non-lethal systems, such as electronic warfare, smoke/obscurants and psyops, are already incorporated into existing doctrine, but new technologies mean that for certain operations doctrine needs to be reconceptualized. Accord-ing to Mazarr, doctrine should constitute fundamental guidance and direction and makes up the fundamental principles by which military forces or elements guide their actions in support of national or trans-national (in the case of the UN) objectives.[4] Development of new military doctrine and appropriate organization enables new technolo-gies to be utilized to their full potential, but historically these two elements have always lagged behind the procurement of new weapons systems. Doctrine should be authoritative but it requires judgement in application (Tritten, 1995, p. 25).

Formulation of doctrine informs planning for research and procurement programmes and therefore the equipping of military forces. A particular service doctrine (e.g. that of an army or air force) indicates to allies and other elements of the armed services broad conceptual aspects of 'how' that element intends to fight (Hall, 1985, p. 33). Non-lethality, which has been described as the theory that overwhelming non-lethal force could be used to defeat lethal force, is achieved by using non-lethal weapons. Doctrine says that non-lethal weapons can be used earlier to: deter by denial in order to support diplomacy; limit aggression; minimize collateral damage and unnecessary casualties by non-lethally disarming or dissuading opponents; destroy lethal capability with a minimum of damage to non-combatants, combatants, and the environment; minimize reconstruction costs; maintain the moral high ground; enforce the rule of law; protect the lives of military and law enforcement agency personnel; offer military and police elements more mission options before having to resort to lethal force (Morris, Morris & Baines, 1995, p. 24).

Since 1989 the context for military planning has changed. As we have already seen in Chapter 1, military analysts such as Mazarr (Mazarr, 1993) and Metz and Kievit (Metz and Kievit, 1994) talk of a Military Technology Revolution (MTR)[5] and a Revolution in Military Affairs (RMA)[6] resulting from innovative technologies, new doctrine, and military restructuring. MTR and RMA are influenced by factors such as defence budgets, defence scenarios, national security and foreign policy interests and commercial and industrial research and development .

Barry et al. (1994) proposed eight doctrinal precepts for non-lethal military means in OOTW. These are:

1. Non-lethal military means can add leverage to diplomacy and economic sanctions towards the accomplishment of political and military objectives.
2. Non-lethal weapons can be most effective in circumstances requiring minimum collateral damage and non-combatant casualties.
3. National and transnational threats can be targeted with non-lethal means.
4. Non-lethal weapons have inherent characteristics of synergism, versatility, and discretion.
5. Non-lethal measures would be most effective if targeted against

the 'centre of gravity' of an adversary in quick, decisive, and concentrated fashion.

6. Like diplomacy and economic sanctions, non-lethal means will be most effective as part of a co-ordinated coalition effort.
7. Non-lethal military means, used in the early stages of a conflict, could limit risk of escalation.
8. Within a given operation, non-lethal means can be employed covertly, overtly, or both.

Strategy and operations

Military forces need to look at strategy that utilizes non-lethal technologies and warfare as an adjunct to conventional and nuclear war. This requires changes to military doctrine and the incorporation of non-lethal weaponry in training, development and acquisition systems (Opall, 1992). It will also be necessary to formulate joint, multi-service, service and combined service doctrines to incorporate non-lethal systems across military services in a co-ordinated and coherent manner.[7] Strategies are often conceived as 'game plans' for achieving desired goals with limited means and as the linking of ends and means – a process that tells how finite resources will be employed to accomplish declared objectives.[8] Variables that affect strategy formulation include: global factors; national interest, considered to be the highest objective; long-term goals, such as freedom of the seas or an open market, versus short-term aims (Bartlett et al., 1995). Non-lethal weapons have important strategic value in that they: (a) expand the set of options available to policy makers and commanders for operations other than war and operations short of war, (b) act as force multipliers in war situations, (c) reduce the costs of conflict across the spectrum, (d) strengthen deterrence by reinforcing flexible response capabilities, (e) maintain the leverage of the US lead in advanced technology (Swett, 1994). Military forces are deployed in a variety of operations which may be simply classified (see Table 3.1).

Non-lethal weapons are used within the context of their offensive and defensive capabilities, and within the two broad categories of warfighting and OOTW. In offensive operations, non-lethal weapons may be used for example to separate combatants and non-combatants; in peacekeeping operations to control crowds and riots; in war fighting to disable or disrupt military logistics and communication systems and to neutralize power supplies, transport and other aspects of civilian and military infrastructure; to spread propaganda and

Table 3.1   Military operations (offensive and defensive)

War fighting	Operations other than war (OOTW)
Global conflict	Sanctions (threats, sanctions)
Regional conflict	Peacekeeping
National defence	Wider peacekeeping
Counter-insurgency	Humanitarian relief
Peace enforcement	Internal policing operations
	Operations against drugs/international terrorism
	Preventing outbreaks of violent conflict
	Military incursions

(mis)information; to disable or destroy weapons of mass destruction; to evacuate non-combatants; to protect humanitarian relief delivery; to help in counter-drug missions; and to enforce economic sanctions by using measures that, for example, rapidly degrade vehicle tyres and lines of communication. In war-fighting scenarios, the effect of non-lethal weapons can be increased when they are used in conjunction with psychological operations and precision delivery systems, and they could also be used as pre-lethal weapons to slow down or disable targets, thus making them easier to hit and destroy. Because the primary intention of the use of non-lethal weapons is not to deliberately permanently injure or maim people, they may be attractive to counter-insurgency operations that have the objective of winning the 'hearts and minds' of local populations because, by using these non-lethal options, less harm is done to the people, the environment and sites of cultural importance.

Non-lethal weapons have utility in defensive measures such as perimeter security for military bases and protection of embassies and other installations in foreign countries. In these cases, the acoustic systems, foam barriers, microwave systems and other temporarily incapacitating substances may be deployed.

> Scientists and military officers insist that new peacekeeping/peace enforcement tactics and weapons can be effective only if merged with comprehensive, advanced information systems. Space, airborne and ground based sensors – including unattended devices – would provide a flood of data that enable decisive actions in non-combat situations. Information must be processed and routed to the proper authorities in time to preclude hostile action, ideally, or to enable rapid response if firing occurs. (Scott, 1995)

Military Experience of Non-Lethal Weapons in Operations

We have chosen four examples to illustrate various scenarios and developmental phases of the operational use of non-lethal weapons, and the controversies that surrounded their use.

1. Northern Ireland in the 1970s represents a violent phase of internal conflict when new non-lethal riot control weapons were seen on the streets of the UK for the first time within the context of the army acting in support of the 'civil power'.
2. In Vietnam, US forces used large amounts of defoliant herbicides and CS gas in a war situation with devastating results.
3. New non-lethal technology was demonstrated during the 1991 Gulf War when coalition forces, under the lead of the US, ejected Iraqi forces from Kuwait and invaded Iraq.
4. In Somalia in 1995, US Marines were equipped with non-lethal weapons when they had the task of protecting the withdrawal of the UNOSOM II peacekeeping force from Mogadishu.

Northern Ireland – British Army

Troops arriving in Northern Ireland in August 1969 were poorly prepared to deal with riots and street battles and were basically equipped with wooden batons and small shields (Barzilay, 1973, p. 69). However, an armoury of riot and crowd control weapons was soon built up, the most extensively used non-lethal weapons being CS gas and various impact weapons such as rubber and plastic bullets and water cannon.

The army had previous experience of using CS gas during the independence struggles in Cyprus in 1958. Although the Royal Ulster Constabulary (RUC) had used CS gas in the Bogside area before the army went in, questions were raised about its effectiveness. When first used, the gas was either fired from a small hand gun or thrown as a grenade, and many cartridges were needed to lay down enough gas to affect the rioters. Also the gas's effectiveness depended on weather conditions – wind could blow the gas away from a riot; rioters also developed a simple gas mask made from handkerchiefs soaked in vinegar water. The army developed a Landrover-mounted elastic catapult system which enabled a larger grenade to be used, at greater distances. A rubber-encased grenade was eventually developed which could be fired from vehicles such as Saracen armoured personnel carriers and Ferret armoured cars. After the grenade's launching, thousands of CS gas pellets burst from inside the rubber case, spreading over a wide area and producing a dense cloud of gas (Barzilay, 1973, p. 70). James Callaghan was the government minister in charge when the Northern Ireland Prime Minister asked permission for the RUC to use CS gas in the face of escalating disturbances. Callaghan reports that he and his colleagues were troubled at that moment because

> 'persuasive attempts were being made on the international scene to outlaw the use of gas, and I certainly had no desire to weaken these attempts'. However, in the absence of more policemen there was a choice of evils. The use of CS gas might enable the RUC to control riots and so obviate the need to call in troops. That, Callaghan says, would have been an advantage in itself.[9]

Callaghan later set up an expert committee under Sir Harold Himsworth to investigate the effects of using gas as a riot control agent.

During the early 1970s in Northern Ireland the British army's riot tactics did not need to take into account the threat from gunmen. When deployed for crowd control, few soldiers had their rifles at the ready, and squads reacted mostly to hand-thrown projectiles such as stones, broken glass and iron piping. These tactics of course had to change because of the dangers of a crowd being used to lure soldiers into the open and so to set them up for a shooting by terrorists or militant paramilitary groups. With experience, the army has developed more sophisticated tactics which include using armoured vehicles for protection (Dewar, 1985, p. 42). In riot situations a space, which is dependent on the range of missiles used by both troops and rioters, is created between both sides, and this makes it difficult for troops and police to arrest leaders of the disturbance. To help overcome this, 'snatch squads' were developed.

Plastic and rubber bullets were used extensively as anti-riot non-lethal weapons in Northern Ireland. These blunt trauma impact weapons were designed to 'maximize pain while constrained to minimize hazard levels'.[10] Rubber bullets, which have been described as the most controversial weapon ever used by the British army, were a development of the wooden 'baton rounds' which were originally used by Hong Kong police in reacting to riots in that British colony. These wooden batons were one-inch-long fluted cylinders made out of teak

and fired from riot or signal guns. They were aimed directly at rioters'
legs or, when fired at close range, onto the ground so that they rico-
cheted into the bodies of rioters; during flight they gave a whistling
sound for extra psychological effect. Later versions were up to 190mm
long, 40mm in diameter, and weighted with a metal core. Because of
the force of impact and the danger of splintering, there was a
possibility that they could cause serious internal injury or death
(Deane-Drummond, 1975, p. 149). In fact a young girl was killed by
one of these wooden baton rounds. Whilst considered appropriate for
use in Hong Kong against Asians, wooden batons were considered
too dangerous to use in Northern Ireland against UK citizens so the
rubber bullet was designed and first used in Northern Ireland in June
1970. The first rubber bullets were blunt-nosed, 150mm long, 40mm
in diameter and 155g in weight. Thousands of rubber and plastic
bullets were used; the official estimates give numbers as follows:[11]

> 1971 – 16,782 rubber bullets
> 1972 – 23,363 rubber bullets
> 1973 – 12,766 rubber bullets
> 1974 – 2,828 rubber and plastic bullets
> 1975 – 3,701 rubber and plastic bullets
> 1976 – 3,464 plastic bullets

Rubber bullets were not very accurate, and serious injuries and
fatalities were recorded not only among people taking part in rioting,
but also among bystanders (Millar et al., 1975; *Jane's Infantry Weapons
1976*, p. 441; Faul and Murray, 1981; Curtis, 1987). A study showed
that one in every 16,500 bullets used in Northern Ireland killed, one
in every 1,900 caused permanent disability, and one in every 800
caused serious injury.[12] So the army acquired the plastic bullet. This
was a flat-ended plastic cylinder which was lighter, more accurate,
and had a longer range than the rubber bullet.

Other non-lethal weapons considered for use in Northern Ireland

Various non-lethal weapons using sound were looked at by the Army.
In January 1973 thirteen Sound Curdler systems were bought from
Applied Electro Mechanics of Alexandria, Virginia, USA (Ackroyd,
1977, p. 224), which had the capability of producing a noise rating
of 120 decibels at thirty feet. The volume of sound produced by this
device, also known as a People Repeller, could cause disorientation
and nausea, and in the opinion of some experts at the time, at close

range could cause permanent damage to hearing. The Sound Curdler could be connected into a highly amplified mobile voice-and-sound transmission system known as the HPS-1 (Applegate, 1969, p. 270) which gave it an effective range of 2½ miles. The HPS-1 was developed to help with voice communication over longer distances in situations such as sieges, riots and battle.

Also in 1973, the *New Scientist* reported that a non-violent ultrasonic crowd dispersal device known as the Squawk Box had been tested in Northern Ireland.[13] According to Rodwell the device emitted:

> two marginally different frequencies, almost out of audible range, through two separate speakers. These combine in the ear to produce two other frequencies – one the sum of the two component frequencies and the other the difference between them. Thus two speakers emitting say 16,000 Hz and 16,002 Hz produce a high frequency in the ear of 32,000 Hz and a low beat of 2 Hz. (*New Scientist*, 20 September 1973, p. 664)

The machine was directional so it could be accurately aimed at individual targets, and the virtual inaudibility of the equipment was said to produce a 'spooky' psychological effect. The British army subsequently denied using the device.

A 'photic driver' was being developed in the early 1970s by Charles Bovill at Allen International with encouragement and support from a 'military neurologist'. The photic driver combined ultrasonic sound (such as that produced by the Squawk Box) and infrared light (modified from stroboscopic lights) so that nothing was seen or heard, with the objective of producing symptoms such as giddiness, nausea, fainting, and throbbing in the ears. There was a fear that, unless carefully controlled, such a device would cause epileptic fits to those who already suffered from them, and could trigger a first seizure in some people. Although the device drew sharp criticism from medical experts, Bovill is reported to have responded with a reference to the 'puke ethics' of his critics.[14] He said that 'coming from a military family, I have seen enough killing and I'd really like to see weapons that don't kill'.[15] He did modify the device to use lower frequency beams, but the photic driver was not used by the British army. A simple way of combating the light effects of the photic driver would be to look away or just cover one eye.[16] There was speculation that the Swedish police were thinking of asking Bovill's help in dealing with a bank siege situation if the gunman could not be flushed out with K62 (the Swedish designation for CS gas). In the event, the gas worked so the photic driver was not required.[17]

Water cannon were used occasionally and the British army experimented with rocket-fired nets for capturing rioters, but the idea did not catch on.

Vietnam War – US forces

The two weapons most extensively used by US forces in Vietnam which fall into the non-lethal category were herbicides and CS gas.

Herbicides

The chemical 245T was originally used as a weapon by the British Army in the late 1940s and early 1950s in Malaya against communist insurgents.[18] The objectives were to deny the enemy cover and to destroy suspected guerrilla food plantations, so as to starve them into submission. In Vietnam, US forces also adopted this approach as one of their strategies against the Viet Cong, but on a vaster scale.[19] In November 1961, Operation Ranch Hand was launched using USAF transport planes especially converted for aerial herbicide spraying and capable of carrying 1,000 gallons per mission. The objectives, similar to those of the British in Malaya, were to deny cover and food, and huge tracts of jungle were sprayed between 1961 and May 1971, when the operation ended. The US government stated that the spraying of food crops and cover was specifically aimed at male Viet Cong soldiers who were in isolation from the local population, and where there was any doubt of this civilians in a target area would be warned in advance and told where they could go to be safe. There was a school of thought that said that one of the real objectives of the operation was indeed to move people out of areas under Viet Cong influence and into areas (such as 'protected hamlets') that were under the control of US and South Vietnamese forces. In the US cover denial programme it has been estimated that 64 million litres of herbicide were dispensed on 1.9 million hectares of forest, while 8 million litres were sprayed on 0.3 million hectares of agricultural land for food denial (ICEUSCI, 1972, p. 1:3). Some opponents of the Vietnam War and the spraying technique used in it coined the term 'ecocide' to describe what was happening. Six chemicals in all were used, designated Agents Green, Pink, Purple, White, Blue and Orange. Agent Orange, which contained small amounts of the highly toxic agent dioxin, is probably the most notorious. By the end of the spraying campaign almost 240 pounds of dioxin had been deposited over Vietnam – a few ounces alone would be enough to destroy the populations of London or New York (Harris and Paxman, 1982, p. 192). The use of herbicides at first sight seemed relatively benign in comparison to the slaughter caused by lethal weapons such as cluster bombs, artillery, land mines, napalm and phosphorous and other anti-personnel weapons (Prokosch, 1995). But great damage was being done both to the environment and to the health of people who were either directly sprayed by the herbicides or ate food from the affected regions. There were also reports of birth defects in newly born children. Some American servicemen who came into direct contact with Agent Orange suffered from an unpleasant skin condition called chloracne. Kitson (Kitson, 1971) questioned the efficacy of defoliation and the destruction of vegetation; he pointed out that after the first spraying the vegetation quickly grew back but if an area was sprayed again, the result was widespread destruction of all woody plants. This was not good in the long term for the environment, and from a military point of view the resulting amount of dead brushwood on the ground offered almost as much cover for the enemy as the original jungle.[20] Aerial spraying is also indiscriminate in its application; weather conditions and inaccurate intelligence may mean that people not associated with the enemy may be affected. There were concerns that a precedent was being set in Vietnam because 'once chemicals become accepted weapons in the arsenals of nations, it may be difficult to draw the line between one chemical and another; between one use of chemicals and another' (A.W. Galston, in Rose, 1968, p. 62).

CS gas

We have already seen how the British Army deployed CS gas in riot and crowd control situations in Northern Ireland. In Vietnam the US forces deployed CS gas (and on occasions DM and CN gas) for war-fighting purposes.

> A major risk in the use of nonlethal weaponry is failure to keep the non-lethal aspect clean, that is free of associations with lethal tactics. Such failure is well illustrated in Vietnam now, where a large amount of riot-control chemicals is being used not to achieve casualty reductions but to root the enemy out of his place of cover and concealment so as to make him an easier target for conventional firepower. The basic argument for the use of nonlethal weapons and their practical applicability will be undercut if the rules for their employment remain uncertain. (Coates, 1970, p. 102)

CS gas was introduced into operations in Vietnam to drive enemy combatants from deep caves, tunnels and bunkers; when the Viet Cong had infiltrated civilian areas; and for use in hostage situations.

Enemy soldiers who were driven out into the open as a result of gas application, and who did not surrender usually resumed hostile actions, so lethal force was the usual sequel to such uses of CS gas by US and allied forces. CS gas was also used to complement lethal force, where the stated primary military concern was to save the lives of non-combatants and allied forces. The use of gas could also make it easier to capture enemy soldiers, thus enabling them to be interrogated for intelligence. Since the use of torture was widespread by all sides during the war, the prospect of capture was one to be resisted. But the use of riot control gases was seen to be better than some alternatives:

> Compared with napalm bombs that incinerate whole villages, or a white phosphorous shell that burns a man to the bone, the temporary disabling gases used in Vietnam seem more humane than horrible. (*Time*, 2 April 1965)

CS gas was dispensed in aerosol form and as solid particles which would then undergo sublimation from solid to gas. A high-speed wind machine called 'Mighty Mite' which held up to 80 pounds (35,500 grams) of CS was often used to disperse the gas in powder form into caves and tunnels whereby a high concentration of the gas could be quickly built up, forcing occupants without gas masks out into the open. With such high concentrations being used there was a danger of death by suffocation. In other cases helicopters would first be sent in spraying gas from dispensers, forcing Viet Cong to the surface, then USAF bombers would saturate the area with high-explosive and cluster bombs, and finally ground troops would go in and mop up any survivors.

Other non-lethal weapons research for use in Vietnam

During this period there was ongoing research into other so-called non-lethal and humane weapons. These included investigation of biological agents such as dengue fever, which has the property of producing incapacitating symptoms for a few days after the victim has been infected, which reduces an enemy's fighting capabilities. Unfortunately for the researchers, dengue is not very infectious and requires sandflies to spread it. Its use is therefore very limited. As the discussants at a conference on chemical and biological weapons concluded in 1968:

> This is one sort of weapon that has achieved a degree of popularity in certain circles on the grounds that it is a humane, non-killing weapon, but

it is hard to put this theory to the test without involving a large number of people. (Rose, 1968, p. 57)

Great interest was shown also by researchers in psychedelic drugs such as LSD and BZ as agents that could demotivate and incapacitate soldiers.[21] There are of course huge problems with means of delivery and the fact that the dose and effect vary between individuals, and for individuals at different times. These variables are also dependent on other factors such as previous experience of drugs, physical and mental health, environment, and availability of treatment. Historically this has meant that despite extensive research LSD and other similar psychochemicals have been viewed as too unpredictable in their effects to be used as weapons. There have been reports of illegal testing of LSD on unsuspecting people by the CIA in particular (Harris and Paxman, 1982, p. 204).

1991 Gulf War – US and Coalition forces

The Gulf War provided an opportunity to demonstrate a generation of weapons systems, particularly the so-called 'smart' weapons developed as a result of the technological revolution of the preceding decade, which were designed to increase accuracy and reduce the risks to air and ground forces delivering them. These systems included non-lethal options such as Tomahawk cruise missiles which deactivated Iraqi power stations by releasing thousands of spools of carbon fibres above the power plants and switching stations. These drifted down onto the electrical components causing short circuits, thus cutting off supplies of electricity. This non-lethal attack had lethal consequences because essential public services such as hospitals and water supplies were disrupted causing, for example, vital life-saving equipment to fail and an increase in public health hazards caused by poor sewage disposal and the lack of safe water to drink. It is interesting to note that in many cases, the coalition forces later repeated attacks on these power plants with high explosives just to make sure that they were really out of action. Rogers (1995) reports that the USA has further refined this non-lethal concept with the development of a Wind Corrected Munitions Dispenser (WCMD) which can be dropped onto a target with great accuracy from altitudes up to 40,000 feet. Detonating near ground level, it bursts open releasing microscopic carbon fibres (far smaller than those used in the Gulf) which can penetrate into virtually anything including computers, vehicle electronics, telecommunications equipment, and electric control panels, causing shorting and thus disruption of power, transport and communications. The effect on the health of people in the target area is not clear; for example, what happens to the lungs when these minute filaments are inhaled? Also employed in the Gulf War, under the aegis of non-lethal weapons, were a range of psychological and electronic warfare techniques. The deployment included units such as the 193rd Special Operations Group whose motto is 'We fire electrons not bullets' (Shukman, 1995). This US Air Force unit operates EC-130E Commando Solo aircraft which are packed full of electronic warfare and propaganda systems, enabling the unit to broadcast TV and radio programmes that can reach just about all TV and radio sets in a war zone, and also to jam or disrupt enemy civil and military transmissions. Millions of leaflets urging and telling Iraqi troops how to surrender were dropped during Operation Desert Storm, with much success. One of the lasting images of that operation was of lines of surrendering Iraqi soldiers clasping these leaflets.

O'Connell and Dillapain (1994, p. 28) point to the utility of non-lethal weapons in US Air Force operations where non-lethal concepts in terms of air force applications do not appear to be a departure from the normal evolution of air power. They give an example in the Gulf War when Iraqi MiG aircraft were parked provocatively, as a baiting tactic, in front of an ancient mosque. To attack such a target with conventional high-explosive bombs was out of the question because of the danger of collateral damage to the Ziggurat temple, which is a revered and respected cultural symbol. O'Connell and Dillapain argue that if alternative non-lethal weapons, such as embrittlement and supercaustic agents, were available to planners then such targets as the MiGs could be attacked using non-lethal weapons guided in by precision systems, with little danger of collateral damage.[22] The delivery of non-lethal weapons may require the formation of specialized squadrons, which could consist of pilotless air vehicles, since the effectiveness of many non-lethal weapons under development requires accurate and close-range application and this increases the risk to air crew. The rapid advances in cruise missile technology, global navigation systems, and intelligence and information gathering capabilities will contribute in the future to reducing these risks, making the non-lethal weapon concept more attractive to planners and field commanders.

1995 Somalia – US Marine Corps[23]

In January 1995 the UN decided to terminate the UNOSOM II mission in Somalia and withdraw the UN peacekeeping force (UNPKF) of Pakistani and Bangladeshi soldiers. To help them do this, a request was made to the USA for military forces to help protect the withdrawing peacekeeping troops. The 1 Marine Expeditionary Force (1 MEF) based at Camp Pendleton, under the command of Lt. Gen. A. Zinni, was ordered to provide the appropriate military elements for what was designated Operation United Shield. During planning stages for United Shield, it was recognized that much of 1 MEF's task would be engaging with hostile unarmed civilians, such as looters and rioters, so the staff of the Tactical Exercise Control Group (TECG) of 1 MEF began to look for the best available crowd control equipment to perform this function. The planners knew that there was a need for weapons that would fill the gap effectively between verbal warnings and the use of deadly force; enquiries about less-lethal systems were made, and the TECG visited Sandia Federal Laboratories and Phillips Laboratories during January 1995 to review and evaluate new non-lethal weapons technology, especially two types of foam designed to immobilize or deter any unarmed but hostile civilians.[24] At the same time a Mobile Training Team (MTT) was formed with the task of designing and conducting training routines for the identified non-lethal weapons which could be implemented by February or early March. All these efforts were co-ordinated with the Marine Corps Experimental Unit. Because of the limited time available for planning the operation, several factors influenced the TECG decisions regarding the appropriateness of non-lethal weapon systems on offer. These were: the availability – they had to be delivered by the end of January; the quantity – there had to be sufficient in stock; the performance in the field; the time needed to train Marines with no previous experience – the NLWs had to be delivered from existing weapons systems that Marines were familiar with. With respect to the last factor, the M203 grenade launcher (which includes the M-16) and the 12-gauge shotgun were both systems familiar to the Marines, and they satisfied the requirement that they could easily be converted back to lethal capabilities. The unit chosen to be trained and equipped with non-lethal weapons was Company 1, Battalion Landing Team (BLT), of the 13th Marine Expeditionary Unit Special Operations Capable – 13th MEU(SOC), which formed the landing force for United Shield.

Table 3.2 NLW equipment acquired for 13th MEU(SOC)

- Sticky foam
- Aqueous foam
- Stinger grenades
- Caltrops
- 40mm Munitions
  - No. 40B stinger cartridges
  - No. 40W wooden baton rounds
  - No. 2504 Tri-flex beanbag rounds
  - No. 40F foam rubber rounds
- 12-Gauge Shotgun Munitions
  - No. 23 beanbag rounds
  - No. 23 rubber pellet cartridges
  - No. 23 wood baton rounds
- Oleoresin Capsicum (OC) Aerosol Pepper Projectors
  Mk4, Mk5, Mk46

Before any new weapons system is acquired it is reviewed under DoD Instruction 5500.15 which checks the legality of each weapon under international law, to ensure that it does not violate US treaty obligations.

The Rules of Engagement (ROE) for United Shield were based on the standard principle of a graduated response, authorizing the use of 'minimum force' necessary to repel attacks or imminent threat of attack, and to ensure the safety of the troops. But the ROE also contained specific restrictions on the use of certain 'crowd control' devices. Lorenz points out that:

> This was based on the assumption that there is a clear-cut distinction between the use of deadly force and all other means of force. This approach is not consistent with the practice in the civilian law enforcement field, where the use of force is viewed as a continuum of action rather than a black or white alternative. (Lorenz, 1995, p. 73)

During United Shield, in which over 2,000 US and Italian Marines were deployed, of the NLWs acquired, there was only limited use of sticky foam and caltrops to enhance barrier systems at night during the final stages of the withdrawal. Despite this limited use of new non-lethal weapon technology the Marines were able to point to several operational lessons for future non-lethal weapon utility. There is a clearly identified requirement for non-lethal weapons in Operations Other Than War, but at the time of United Shield most were still under development and few were actually available for operational deployment in sufficient quantities. NLWs are not cheap – Lorenz quotes a single 40mm wood baton round as costing $25 – but the cost must be balanced against the danger of a lethal response if the non-lethal option was not available. Marines felt that the guidelines concerning the distinction between deadly force and non-lethal responses were unrealistic operationally. The use of some NLWs was apparently restricted to situations where deadly force was authorized. One operator is quoted on this:

> If I have to wait until deadly force is authorized before I can shoot them with a bean bag or rubber bullet, why would I resort to less-lethal means at all? (Lorenz, 1995, p. 75)

Behind the Pentagon caution was the worry that some non-lethal weapon systems may turn out to be lethal. For example, it was thought that the sticky foam could suffocate people if sprayed over their heads. In fact the most effective use of such a foam, in the Marines' opinion, is not as an anti-personnel weapon, but rather to supplement barbed wire or other barriers. There are several associated complications with both these scenarios. If foam was used as an anti-personnel weapon, there was a chance of US personnel who came into contact with the 'target' also becoming tangled up. There was also concern that when sticky foam is used to supplement barbed or razor wire barriers, people becoming stuck and then struggling on the wire could seriously injure themselves:

> If the sticky foam had been used to cover unattended portions of barbed wire during the night, in the morning we could have found a dozen Somali youths stuck to the wire, entangled in a bloody trap. Removing the trespassers from the wire would be difficult and not play well on the CNN. (Lorenz, 1995, p. 76)

The viability of the use of non-lethal weapons in Somalia has been questioned. Allen Holmes, US Assistant Secretary of Defense for Special Operations and Low Intensity Conflict, stated that it would not be appropriate at that time to use radical new designs in non-lethal technology until they had been properly tested. He said, 'I think there has been some misinformation about non-lethal weapons. These are not a substitute for the normal suite of weapons available to the US military. They are an adjunct, and they were seen as that when deployed in Somalia.'[25] But Lt. Gen. Anthony Zinni, a supporter of NLWs, said that new technology gave him the flexibility to operate in environments like Somalia more effectively. The Marine Corps commandant, General Charles Krulak, said that an initial concern among some marine commanders that non-lethal weapons would make the troops 'soft' proved unnecessary. The Marines didn't seem any less ready to use lethal force if required to do so (Capaccio, 1995a). In supporting the 1996 Senate authorization language allocating $37.2 million for non-lethal weapons, Krulak wrote to Republican Senator Robert Smith:

> Our experience in Somalia with nonlethal weapons offered ample testimony to the tremendous flexibility they offer to warriors on the field of battle. Their use better enables us to respond proportionately and with greater flexibility to the wide range of threats we can expect to face today and in the future (Morris and Morris, 1995)

The fact that the Marines were enthusiastic about NLWs had a positive influence on other armed services. The US Marine Corps drew up a list of do's and don'ts for the use of less-lethal weapons (Jannery, 1995) which proposed among its guidelines that no marine should be put at risk in an attempt to employ non-lethal means, that less lethal means should not be used in lethal situations, that units using less lethal means should always be covered with lethal weapons as back-up, and that NLWs should not be used just to use them. Many in the US armed services thought it was important not to have an announced policy that would give intelligence to an enemy, allowing development of countermeasures. In the conclusion to his paper Lorenz reiterates:

> Technology is important, but useless without effective training. Doctrine needs to be developed and kept free of complex rules and restrictions. (Lorenz, 1995, p. 76)

In a later paper, Becker and Heal (1996), drawing on the Somalia experience, elaborate the doctrine, strategy and tactics needed for the effective use of non-lethal weapons by peacekeeping forces. Like Lorenz they point out the need for rules of engagement that allow less lethal tactics to include a 'seamless sliding scale of force options' integrating lethal and less lethal options. It is not appropriate just to put non-lethal weapons under the same rules of engagement as lethal weapons. They argue that non-lethal weapons can be used under less restrictive rules of engagement in response to less provocation, so that they can be used sooner in riot situations, thus breaking the cycle of escalation at an earlier stage. It is also vital that peacekeepers understand the dynamics of riot control, have a sound riot control doctrine, and have some understanding of the deeper reasons why people may have become involved in the disturbance. Otherwise there is a danger that peacekeeping forces, instead of remaining the solution, become part of the problem themselves. Becker and Heal also recognize that the technological aspect is not the most important in a low-lethality programme:

> A better approach to less-lethal capability – rather than viewing it as a technology, or group of technologies – is to see it philosophically as a process of de-escalation through early intervention by means of an escalating force continuum. (Becker and Heal, 1996, p. 63)

Fears have been voiced about the danger of some ex-soldiers who have been deployed with NLWs suffering from what is known as 'veteranitis', that is, blaming future ill-health on the use of these weapons. Others have advocated the need for therapy to allay the fears of those hit by these 'new' weapons.

Civilian Police Force Perspectives

Operations in which police forces could use non-lethal weapons cover a broad spectrum of situations. As in military operations, weapons would be chosen according to the specific situation and other enforcement methods being used. These include general police work such as: general protection of life and property (including protection of VIPs); control and dispersion of riots (including prevention of looting); crowd control at public events; arrest of law breakers (including stop-and-search, and close proximity arrest); stopping vehicles involved in crimes; evacuation in situations of natural and man-made disasters; crime prevention; hostage and terrorist incidents; and urban insurgency. Some of these situations may require co-operation with the army and special forces.

Applegate (1969) described in some detail the non-lethal weapons available to US law enforcement agencies for use in riot control situations during the 1960s, and the operational tactics required then for the control and dispersal of mobs and crowds. These included chemical agents and acoustic devices, some of which we have already described in the context of military use, and also more specialized equipment. In the early days of the US civil rights movement, police used electric cattle prods to break up demonstrations and protests but this practice, quite rightly, quickly drew heavy criticism from civil liberties and human rights groups. However, high-voltage electric shock devices such as the Shock Baton were developed and used indiscriminately, especially on black protesters in the southern states (Coates, 1972, p. 55). These weapons, based around a Tesla coil, could deliver a high-voltage, low-amperage shock which the makers claimed was no worse to the victim than a powerful bee sting, but not as severe. The effect of these weapons was described as:

> psychological as well as physical. Almost all people have an instinctive dislike and fear of electricity and the shock effect which it produces, and will retreat when in this danger. (Applegate, 1969, p. 253)

There was general public repugnance at the use of this weapon (which the police defended on the grounds that it was safer to disable someone using this device than to hit them with a baton), and its use became more restricted to, for example, maintaining control in prisons. Coates (1972) reported several other electrical innovations at this time. The German police had an armoured personnel carrier, with a high-voltage gate-like attachment on the front, designed to clear streets of demonstrators; a device was patented that projected two electrically charged water streams, one positive and one negative, which would meet at the target thus closing the circuit and producing an electric shock; an electrified police jacket to repel assailants was developed; and another innovation was a Taser weapon which fired small electric barbs designed to catch in clothing and paralyse the victim until the current was switched off. It was thought that the Taser-type weapon, which was capable of delivering a 50,000-volt pulse at two-millionths of an amp 12–14 times a second, could find utility, for example, in aircraft hijacking situations. There were seen to be several disadvantages with Tasers, however. They were single-shot weapons with a limited range whose effectiveness could be hindered by a victim's heavy clothing, by people who might be psychologically and emotionally disturbed, and by people under the influence of drugs. Another danger identified by US police was the use of the Taser near water, and in one case a man who had doused himself with gasoline died from a fire caused when a Taser was used (Sweetman, 1987, p. 4). An electrified glove, the Talon, with an electrical pulse generator in the palm and bottom side of the fingers was also being manufactured.

At a major review conference convened by the US Attorney General in June 1986, recommendations concerning policy and operational requirements for law enforcement agencies were put forward (Sweetman, 1987). These included the requirement that the development and acquisition of non-lethal weapons should be carefully matched to operational needs; that police officers should be convinced that the NLW was effective, reliable and practical; that NLWs were adequately tested; that there were guidelines for the use of NLWs, and controls against their abuse; that there should be more co-operation between researchers, law enforcement agencies and manufacturers in the development of NLWs; that legal liability issues needed to be examined.

In 1995 the NASA-sponsored National Technology Transfer Center and the US Justice Department's National Institute of Justice (NIJ) formed a joint project with the objectives of (1) looking for technologies in the private sector, academia and federal agencies that had application to fighting crime, and (2) commercializing US government technologies coming out of laboratories such as Sandia National Laboratories and the Idaho National Engineering Laboratory that would have application with law enforcement agencies (Lessard, 1995). The programme, which was managed by Nick Montanarelli at the NIJ Office of Law Enforcement and Technology Commercialization, was allocated a budget of $1.5 million for the fiscal year 1995, with a 'sizeable increase' promised for 1996.[26]

Specific non-lethal weapons are appropriate for particular law enforcement situations, giving a spectrum of tactical options allowing for distraction, disorientation, dispersal, and immobilization or incapacitation (Sweetman, 1987, p. 14). NLWs for use by police officers should have minimal side effects; affect only the offender; have a rapid but temporary effect; be durable to withstand a rugged operational environment; be portable with minimum effect on the movement of the police officer; fire more than once without reloading; be operable with one hand; and be difficult for an assailant to gain control of.

In the mid-1990s, UK police forces were showing an increasing interest in non-lethal weapons as part of their Personal Protection Programme.[27] Police officers were already equipped with body armour and extendible batons and Sir Paul Condon, the Metropolitan Police Commissioner, requested the evaluation and testing of 'pepper spray' incapacitants to help police officers restrain violent individuals.[28] Pepper sprays had previously been rejected by the

Table 3.3   NLWs appropriate for policing operations

Vehicles
- Armoured for protection
- As platforms for water cannon, electric shock dischargers, gas application

Personal protection
- Shields (including electric shields)
- Body armour
- Helmets
- Batons
- Chemicals (Mace,[29] 'pepper' gases)
- Electric shock devices (batons and jackets)
- Self-defence training (e.g. choke holds)
- Negotiation and mediation techniques

Riot control and arrest
- Gases (CN, CS, pepper)
- Obscuring smokes
- Batons (short and long extendible)
- Electrical devices
- Sound devices (flash-bang grenades, Curdler, Squawk Box)
- Bright and flashing lights (strobe/photic driver)
- Chemical barriers (foam barriers, sticky nets, slippery substances)
- Barbed wire
- Rifle-launched projectiles (rubber and plastic bullets, beanbag projectiles, dye marker pellets)
- Dart guns (tranquillizers)

Monitoring and restraint[30]

Others
- Video recording (acts as a non-lethal deterrent by recording events and evidence)

Home Secretary, Michael Howard, because of the severe effects caused by this substance. These include temporary blindness, a burning sensation on the skin, upper body spasms and breathing difficulties. Research by the US Army in 1993 had concluded that pepper gas could also cause mutagenic effects, carcinogenic effects, sensitization, cardiovascular and pulmonary toxicity as well as possible human fatalities. In the USA, 61 deaths had been reported that were associated with police use of pepper gas (Ballantyne, 1996). By early 1996 and within the context of an increasing number of violent attacks on police officers in the UK, the calls for the introduction of CS gas sprays for personal protection became louder. The Home Secretary approved police trials for CS spray to begin with 2,000 police in sixteen regional police forces in March 1996; the sprays were seen as a halfway measure between baton and firearm. Whilst welcoming these trials, the Police Federation still expressed a preference for pepper sprays (Campbell, 1996). Arguments were made for and against the introduction of CS gas at this operational level. From the perspective of the police officer they provided a quick-acting incapacitating agent which offered protection and aided in arrest situations, kept violent assailants at a distance and when used correctly should result in less harm to the attacker than if the police officer used a baton or firearm. Opponents of CS sprays pointed out that there were health risks, that there was a danger of the sprays being used routinely for offensive purposes as well as for defensive reasons, and that it was another step in the increasing militarization of police forces. The term 'war against crime' was coming to mean exactly that. There would need to be thorough independent monitoring of the use of the CS, and police officers were instructed that they could only use the gas if there was a genuine threat of violent attack. For some researchers the whole programme had even more sinister implications:

> There is a danger that the multi-national merchants marketing new pepper gas technical fixes will push ever more alien gassing devices – such as temporarily blinding pepper foam – on to an unwilling British public. Dealing with vicious thugs is one matter, but already manufacturers and suppliers are producing back pack sprays for mass public order control on the streets and in prisons. (Ballantyne, 1996)

However, sincere visible and determined efforts by the police to reduce both the level of police violence and police resort to lethal force should help to improve their image and promote good public relations. But there are legal implications in that misuse of gas sprays can provoke litigation from the victim, and medical conditions that arise at a later date may be blamed on the use of a non-lethal weapon. One police officer who was involved in the early testing of the CS spray decided to sue for compensation after his eyes were damaged in such a test. Controversy around the trial of CS gas sprays was compounded when the police were called to a domestic dispute in

London involving a Ghanaian-born asylum seeker and his wife. During his arrest a violent struggle took place and CS spray was used. On arrival at the police station the man collapsed and later died; a post-mortem showed he had a hypertensive heart condition. There were immediate calls by groups such as the civil rights group Liberty for the trials to be halted until it could be ascertained that the CS gas spray, which some monitoring groups claimed was five times stronger than that used in the USA, was not the primary cause of death. A police spokesman stated:

> There is no evidence to suggest the CS spray contributed to this tragic death. There are no plans to suspend use of this spray, which has been used on more than 20 occasions so far and we are not aware of any cases of long-term adverse reactions. (Younge, 1996)

Associated with an apparent increase in criminal activity is a rise in the prison population and the related cost to taxpayers in maintaining and improving the prison system. To help reduce this burden, electronic monitoring schemes have been developed which enable thousands of offenders to be kept under house arrest and out of prison. These 'home arrest' systems monitor an offender's movements and automatically notify a police station if the electronic tag wearer moves out of his or her home. It has been proposed that this monitoring and surveillance system could be extended into one that incorporates a non-lethal restraining capacity as well. For example, if the offender attempted to move out of his prescribed area of house arrest or if he violated parole conditions, a signal would be sent to the electronic receiver attached to the offender, and a 'zap of electricity' of enough force to immobilize the wearer temporarily would be delivered (Hoshen et al., 1995). The implications of this type of social control are enormous.

Conclusion

Again the point must be made that there is no such thing as a truly non-lethal weapon. Chemical agents, electric shocks, directed energy beams, optical and acoustic stimulation can all prove fatal. But as we have seen there are situations in war fighting, riot control, hostage rescue and peacekeeping operations when non-lethal options, which fall between lethal and completely 'non-violent' options, have a place and offer police and military forces a greater range of options before they have to resort to the use of lethal force.

Whilst there is considerable potential for dual-use technology transfer and operational development opportunities in the development of NLWs for both military and civil law enforcement requirements, a clear distinction must be kept between these two elements. For economic reasons alone it makes sense to both politicians and the agencies for joint development work to be undertaken. But the distinction between military and policing actions is becoming blurred, and the equipment needed by military units sometimes has much in common with that of civil police engaged in crowd and riot control. There are also dangers in any overenthusiastic transfer of military technologies to civil police forces. Acknowledging this, the US Attorney-General Janet Reno said the following in 1994, when talking of plans for a partnership between the DoD and DoJ to develop dual-use non-lethal weapons systems through a Center for Defense and Law Enforcement Technology:

> When the police use these devices [originally conceived for the military] they must be constrained by the knowledge that the people they are restraining aren't enemies; they are fellow citizens, with a full set of civil rights. (quoted in Pemberton, 1994)

There were plans for a Community Acceptance Panel whose membership would include the American Civil Liberties Union, the National Association for the Advancement of Colored People and Handgun Control Inc., but critics said that instead of asking questions about the ethics of introducing these new weapons at all, the panel would be determining how to get the public to accept them.

As we have noted, the concept of non-lethality is not new, and various non-lethal weapons have been used throughout history in war fighting and in policing. In 1970 Coates investigated potential non-lethal mechanisms and recommended that more research was needed in this area to minimize destruction and fatalities in future overseas urban operations in which the USA was likely to become involved. He correctly identified the US military as becoming increasingly involved in roles that could be classified as benign and quasi-combat such as disaster relief, peacekeeping and evacuation. Weapons that once were considered exotic or the stuff of science fiction have become, or are now becoming, operational possibilities because of technological advances and the type of conflict situations that are now being encountered by police and military forces. The speed of these developments left doctrine, strategy and policy processes struggling to keep pace. It is unlikely (although an objective worth striving for) that non-lethal weapons will ever replace lethal weapons, and most military planners do not now see them in isolation but as part of an integrated strategy and doctrine. Most soldiers just see non-lethal weapons as another weapons system.

> Whatever utility less-deadly arms – crowd control techniques, really – may boast in future US engagements overseas, clearly, the ultimate big stick will remain high-velocity metal fragments that remorselessly slice and dice. (Morrison, 1995)

Notes

1. Lamb was Director of Policy Planning Special Operations/Low Intensity Conflicts, US Department of Defense.

2. The Council for Foreign Relations is a non-profit, non-partisan membership organization with the aims of improving the understanding of US foreign policy and international affairs. It sponsors study programmes and meetings, and publishes *Foreign Affairs*.

3. For the debate, see for example, Doswald-Beck, ed. (1993); Human Rights Watch (1995a and 1995b).

4. Mazarr (1993). 'In an ideal world, doctrine would be developed first and inform all other decisions, dictating what kinds of military forces need to be deployed and what equipment they require. Of course, the process is interactive: only by knowing what technologies will be available, both now and in the future, can the authors of doctrine know what other forces might be capable of and devise tactics to take advantage of those capabilities.'

5. MTR is a fundamental advance in technology, doctrine, or organization that renders existing methods of conducting warfare obsolete. An advance is also revolutionary when it exercises a critical effect on some fundamental aspect of strategy (Mazarr, 1993, p. 16).

6. *Armed Forces Journal International*, May 1995, pp. 38–9.

7. See Tritten (1995) for an exploration of US military doctrine.

8. Bartlett et al. (1995).

9. From J. Callaghan, *A House Divided*, Collins, London, 1973, p. 29. Quoted in *New Scientist*, 6 September 1973. At that time the RUC only had the older and more dangerous CN gas.

10. D.O. Egner, E.B. Shank, M. Wargovitch and A.F. Tiedemann, *A Multidisciplinary Technique for the Evaluation of Less Lethal Weapons, Vol.1*, Aberdeen, Md: US Army Land Warfare Laboratory, 1973. Quoted in Ackroyd et al. (1973), p. 207.

11. Quoted in Faul and Murray (1981), p. 5.

12. *New Scientist*, 20 September 1973, p. 668.

13. See articles by Robert Rodwell in *New Scientist*, 20 September 1973, p. 684, and 27 September 1973, p. 730.

14. Ackroyd et al. (1977), p. 226.

15. *New Scientist*, 29 March 1973, p. 726.

16. *New Scientist*, 11 October 1973, p. 115.

17. *New Scientist*, 6 September 1973, p. 575.

18. 245T is Trichlorophenoxyacetic acid.

19. A summary of the defoliant programme undertaken in the Vietnam War can be found in Rose,1968, Chapter 5 by A.W. Galston: 'Defoliants'.

20. Nowadays, new sensing technologies enable the movement of troops and material to be discovered even in deep cover.

21. Such drugs are also known as psychomimetics and hallucinogens.

22. O'Connell and Dillapain do point out the broader general sensitivity of attack on targets in close vicinity to monuments and buildings, particularly those of cultural and religious symbolic importance.

23. This section has drawn heavily on an article by Colonel Frederick Lorenz, 'Less-Lethal Force in Operation United Shield', *Marine Corps Gazette*, September 1995.

24. Whilst the terms 'non-lethal', 'less-lethal', 'less than lethal', and 'limited effects technology' were used during the operation, the Marines preferred to use less-lethal to describe a system 'that is not intended to be lethal when correctly employed'.

25. Interview in *Defense News*, 24–30 April 1995, p. 30.

26. Montanarelli had previously worked for ARPA's Technology Reinvestment Project, and also had a background in law enforcement. Lessard reports that he helped develop the concept of lightweight body armour and did a lot of work on walk-through stations to prevent airline hijackings.

27. Protection was also needed from criminals, such as football hooligans and robbers, who already had access to and were using CS gas.

28. Valerie Elliot, *Sunday Telegraph*, 18 June 1995.

29. Applegate (1969), p. 197. Chemical mace – a liquid, long-range, selective gas projector with a repeat capacity and containing low concentrations of CN tear gas formula – was first used as an individual police non-lethal weapon in the USA in 1965.

30. Hoshen et al. (1995).

4

Controls and Constraints: Legal and Ethical Dilemmas

In this chapter we will consider the general principles of the international law of armed conflict, and the legal and ethical aspects of the usage of non-lethal weapons with respect to national and international laws and conventions, matters of conscience, and the dangers of their use to human life. There is a vast literature associated with this complex subject, which we will only touch on, and we would refer the reader to this for specialist and detailed information. Useful starting points include Best, 1983; Goldblat, 1995; ICRC, 1993 and 1994; Kalshoven, 1987 and 1990; Roberts, and Guelff, 1989; and SIPRI, 1976. Several fundamental questions must be asked because of fears that NLWs may contravene ethical and legal rules or guidelines concerning the prohibition of the use of methods or means of warfare of a nature to cause unnecessary suffering or superfluous injury. These concerns must be placed within the context of the claim that NLWs in fact offer more humane alternatives for war fighting and civil policing, and that NLWs have an acceptably low probability of inflicting permanent disablement on personnel (1994, US DoD NLW Draft Policy). Two questions need to be asked (Greenwood in Doswald-Beck, ed., 1993, pp. 71–82): first, whether the use of NLWs would be contrary to existing principles of international law regarding the use of conventional weapons; and, second, whether there is a case for devising a new measure that would specifically regulate the use of these weapons on the battlefield (or elsewhere).

The discussion in this chapter recognizes that all weapons can cause suffering and that all weapons can be used indiscriminately and inappropriately. Military commanders want to maximize weapons capabilities so that quicker and easier victories ensue. Police wish to arrest criminals with as little danger as possible to themselves and the criminal. But weapons now available as a result of new technology offer new scope for violation and reinterpretation of the existing laws and norms. The weakness of treaties is that they are only applicable to other signatories or allies of those signatories, and that multilateral conventional arms control agreements are difficult to police and enforce. Associated questions that must be asked when looking at the legal and ethical perspectives include:

- Do NLWs have functions that are particularly unacceptable?
- Do NLWs help to 'humanize' war, making it more acceptable?
- How much consideration do policy makers give to whether world and domestic public opinion thinks that a particular weapon is inhumane (the campaigns against land mines and laser weapons in the 1990s, for example)?
- Does the military always reveal explicitly the potential of weapons systems to politicians, and do they always get clearance from political authority to use particular weapons? On first presentation some NLWs do not appear to be obviously weapons that could be classed as inhumane.
- Do NLWs weaken or strengthen existing treaties?
- Can they offer alternatives to existing lethal weaponry to allow states space seriously to consider forms of conventional disarmament?

It is not the assumption of this chapter that all NLWs fall into the 'unacceptable to use' category and should be outlawed, but experience has shown that beneficial claims for new weapons systems must be carefully examined. On occasions, more sinister aspects of such systems have been hidden from public scrutiny. Some writers have claimed that powerful forces are at work to diminish the humanitarian perspective in policy making (Krepon, 1974, p. 605). In a paper that examined 'area weapons' and one type in particular, the Cluster Bomb Unit (CBU), Krepon states:

> Policy assumptions, bureaucratic behaviour, and political imperatives all work to dehumanize in the abstract; when placed in the context of weapons development and use during wartime, they become brutally real. This is especially true when area weapons are billed as life-savers to American infantrymen and pilots. The nature of the bureaucratic war machine does the rest – it minimizes responsibility while maximizing the possibilities of wide-scale damage to save American lives. (Krepon, 1974, p. 605)

Krepon gives four guidelines to help inform whether weapons will contravene humanitarian perspectives: (1) Get political input on weapons development from the start; (2) Evaluate collateral damage possibilities of weapons as they are developed; (3) Prepare guidelines for anti-personnel weapons' use prior to engagement; (4) Conduct field checks once weapons are operational. Such guidelines would enable NLWs to be continually monitored by both civilian and military analysts. Specifically it could be noted if their use changed, pressures on field commanders could mean a temptation to utilize weapons in such a manner as to contravene inhumane weapons conventions.

Principles of Law

Certain general principles of international law regarding conventional weaponry have evolved, and the international community has adopted a number of specific prohibitions or restrictions, each of which deals with the use of a particular type of weapon or method of warfare. These principles can be broadly categorized as those that come under the Law of Armed Conflict and those that come under the remit of Principles Governing Weapons.

Law of armed conflict

The concept of *proportionality* accepts that all weapons and military action can cause suffering, but states that any suffering caused must be balanced against *military necessity*. Proportionality is embraced within the general concept of *humanity* which demands that combatants and non-combatants should not be subjected to unnecessary suffering, for example a wound should be inflicted to heal as painlessly as possible (Cook et al., 1995, p. 80). These terms are of course open to wide interpretation.

Principles concerning weapons

Greenwood (in Doswald-Beck, ed., 1993, pp. 72–3) has identified three general principles governing the prohibition and control of weapons, the 'unnecessary suffering' principle, the 'discrimination' principle, and the 'treachery or perfidy' principle. Before reviewing some of the international control and prohibition treaties, declarations and conventions that may impact on non-lethal weapons, it is worth clarifying these important terms.

(1) The '*unnecessary suffering*' principle prohibits the use of methods or means of warfare calculated to cause unnecessary suffering or superfluous injury (Hague Regulations, Article 23(e); Protocol 1, Article 35(2)). The 'unnecessary suffering' principle provides a legal and ethical base line against which the utility of weapons can be judged, and it has acted as a stimulus for specific bans on particular weapons such as explosive or inflammable bullets, soft-headed (dumdum) bullets, poison gas, and weapons that injure with fragments that cannot be detected by x-rays. The speed of modern technology has enabled the research and development of weapons, including those in the non-lethal group, to be offered to armies and law enforcement agencies, often without the time to develop doctrine, policy and ethical guidelines for their use with respect to the various principles and legal requirements of the laws of war and international humanitarian law.

(2) The '*discrimination*' principle prohibits the use of methods or means of warfare that cannot be directed against a specific military objective and are thus of a nature to strike military objectives and civilians or civilian objectives without distinction (Protocol 1, Article 51(4)). All weapons can be used indiscriminately but some, such as many bacteriological weapons, are incapable of being aimed at military objectives alone (Blix, 1974, p. 26). A problem with NLWs is that they may fall into the dual-use category, and that because of their 'adjustable' capacity to kill, their utility in warfare or law enforcement situations may not be focused. Article 51 of the *Geneva Convention, Additional Protocol 1*, articulates the term 'indiscriminate' as follows:

Para 4 Indiscriminate attacks are prohibited. Indiscriminate attacks are:

(a) those which are not directed at a specific military objective;
(b) those which employ a method or means of combat which cannot be directed at a specific military objective; or
(c) those which employ a method or means of combat the effects of which cannot be limited as required by this Protocol; and consequently, in such case, are of a nature to strike military objectives and civilians or civilian objects without distinction.

Para 5 Among others, the following types of attacks are to be considered as indiscriminate:

(a) an attack by bombardment by any methods or means which treats as a single military objective a number of clearly separated and distinct

military objectives located in a city, town, village or other area containing a similar concentration of civilians or civilian objects; and
(b) an attack which may be expected to cause incidental loss of civilian life,
injury to civilians, damage to civilian objects, or a combination thereof,
which would be excessive in relation to the concrete and direct military
advantage anticipated.

(3) The '*treachery* or *perfidy*' principle prohibits certain perfidious uses
of weaponry and may also prohibit weapons that are inherently
perfidious, although the limits of this principle are far from certain
(Hague Regulations, Article 23 (b)).

In addition to these three general principles, it is important to bear
in mind the provisions of the 'Martens Clause', contained in the
Preamble to the *Hague Convention No. IV*, 1907,

> Until a more complete code of laws of war has been issued, the High
> Contracting Parties deem it expedient to declare that, in cases not in-
> cluded in the Regulations adopted by them, the inhabitants remain under
> the protection and the rule of the principles of the law of nations, as they
> result from the usages established among civilised peoples, from the laws
> of humanity, and the dictates of the public conscience.

Roberts and Guelff (1989, p. 4) make the point that the Martens
Clause is not merely of historical interest because a significant part
of the law of war continues to be in the form of customary principles;
perhaps the most fundamental customary principle is that the right
of conflicting parties to use any means of injuring the enemy is not
unlimited. The same principle is contained in the Geneva Conventions, Protocol 1, Article 1 (2) of 1977, in the following terms:

> In cases not covered by this Protocol or by other international agreements,
> civilians and combatants remain under the protection and authority of the
> principles of international law derived from established custom, from the
> principles of humanity and from the dictates of public conscience.

There are a number of declarations and conventions within whose
framework non-lethal weapons should be considered, with particular
reference to the principles of discrimination and unnecessary suffering.
They set legal and ethical precedents that have relevance for current
and future non-lethal weapons such as lasers, directed energy weapons,
high-power microwaves and infrasound, weapons developed from
biotechnology and genetic engineering, and chemical and biological
weapons. In the next section we will review the more important of
these conventions.

Table 4.1   Summary of declarations and conventions with particular implications for NLWs

---

- The Lieber Code – 1863
- Declaration of St Petersburg – 1868
- Hague Declaration (IV, 2) Concerning Asphyxiating Gases – 1899
  Hague Declaration (IV, 3) Concerning Expanding Bullets – 1899
  Hague Convention (IV) Respecting the Laws and Customs of War on Land – 1907
  (Martens Clause, contained in the Preamble to Hague Convention No. IV – 1907)
- The Protocol for the Prohibition of the Use in War of Asphyxiating, Poisonous or Other Gases, and of Bacteriological Methods of Warfare – 1925
- Geneva Conventions – 1949
- Convention on the Prohibition of the Development, Production and Stockpiling of Bacteriological (Biological) and Toxin Weapons and on their Destruction – 1972
- Convention on the Prohibition of Military or Any Other Hostile Use of Environmental Modification Techniques – 1977
- Geneva Conventions, Additional Protocols I and II – 1977
- Convention on Prohibition or Restrictions on the Use of Certain Conventional Weapons which May Be Deemed to Be Excessively Injurious or to Have Indiscriminate Effects (also known as the UN Inhumane Weapons Convention – UNWC) – 1980
- Chemical Weapons Convention – 1993

Declarations and Conventions

The main declarations and conventions with particular implications for non-lethal weapons are listed in Table 4.1. It is useful to explore aspects of these that help inform and evaluate whether NLWs may contravene the generally accepted restrictions on weapons that kill and maim.

Efforts have been made throughout history to control weapons of war that were thought to be inhumane. Goldblat (1978, p. 211) records the attempt by the Second Lateran Council, 1139, to ban the use of the crossbow between Christians (it was all right to use it against 'infidels'). But Richard I failed to distinguish between infidels and the French so the ban did not become effective. In the 1860s, weapons technology produced exploding bullets. These rifle-fired projectiles had the potential of causing excessive suffering and injury to troops, and they prompted the first effective prohibition of inhumane weapons. Explosive bullets had been used in the American Civil War and by the British in India against 'hard' targets, and experiments were under way to modify them for use against soft (human) targets. In 1868 the Russian government, concerned that such weapons would be routinely used against troops, convened an International Military Commission. As a result of the general feeling of abhorrence for these weapons, the *Declaration of St Petersburg* (1868) was signed which determined to legally prohibit the use of certain weapons. The declaration (in part) stated:

> Considering that the progress of civilization should have the effect of alleviating, as much as possible, the calamities of war:
>   That the only legitimate object which states should endeavour to accomplish during war is to weaken the military force of the enemy;
>   That for this purpose, it is sufficient to disable the greatest possible number of men;
>   That this object would be exceeded by the employment of arms which uselessly aggravate the sufferings of disabled men, or render their death inevitable;
>   That the employment of such arms would, therefore, be contrary to the laws of humanity;...

The declaration prohibited the use of any projectile of less than 400g weight, that was explosive, or that had been coated or had had added to it 'fulminating or inflammable substances'. Looking to future technological developments, a clause was also added which sought 'in view of future improvements which may be effected in the armament of troops, [in order] to maintain the principles which they have established, and to reconcile the necessities of war with the laws of humanity'. In 1863, a few years before the Declaration of St Petersburg, the Lieber Code, which is considered to be the cornerstone of humanitarian law, was drawn up. This established that military necessity does not include means and methods of warfare that are cruel, and that military necessity does take into account the long-term consequences of the use of a particular weapon (Human Rights Watch Arms Project, September 1995). Inspired by the St Petersburg Declaration, later declarations that reflected a recognition of the dangers of inhumane weapons included the following:

Declaration (IV, 2) Concerning Asphyxiating Gases (signed at The Hague 29 July 1899, and entered into force 4 September 1900): contracting parties agree to abstain from the use of projectiles the sole object of which is the diffusion of asphyxiating or deleterious gases.

Declaration (IV, 3) Concerning Expanding Bullets (signed at The Hague 29 July 1899, and entered into force 4 September 1900): contracting parties agree to abstain from the use of bullets that expand or flatten in the human body, such as bullets with a hard envelope which does not entirely cover the core or is pierced with incisions.

The annex to *Convention (IV) Respecting the Laws and Customs of War on Land* (signed at The Hague on 18 October 1907, and entered into force 26 January 1910) declared that it was especially forbidden to employ arms, projectiles, or material calculated to cause unnecessary suffering (Article 23).

The experience of weapons of large-scale destruction and terror in the First World War (especially the widespread and indiscriminate use of poison gases), and the continuing and rapid development of new weapons of mass destruction (chemical, biological and nuclear) prompted the international community to design treaties to prohibit their future use. These included the following:

The Protocol for the Prohibition of the Use in War of Asphyxiating, Poisonous or Other Gases, and of Bacteriological Methods of Warfare (signed at Geneva 17 June 1925, and entered into force 8 February 1928). This stated:

> Whereas the use in war of asphyxiating, poisonous or other gases, and of all analogous liquids, materials or devices, has been justly condemned by the general opinion of the civilized world; and
>
> Whereas the prohibition of such use has been declared in Treaties to which the majority of Powers of the world are Parties; and
>
> To the end that this prohibition shall be universally accepted as a part of International law, binding alike conscience and the practice of nations;
>
> Declare: That the High Contracting Parties, so far as they are not already Parties to Treaties prohibiting such use, accept this prohibition, agree to extend this prohibition to the use of bacteriological methods of warfare.

UN Joint Statement of Agreed Principles for Disarmament Negotiations (made on 20 September 1961). The USA and USSR gave a set of principles as the basis for future multilateral negotiations on disarmament (Goldblat, 1978, p. 75).

Convention on the Prohibition of the Development, Production and Stockpiling of Bacteriological (Biological) and Toxin Weapons and on Their Destruction (signed 10 April 1972, entered into force 26 March 1975). Parties to the convention undertook never in any circumstances to develop, produce, stockpile or otherwise acquire or retain (Article 1):

1. Microbial or other biological agents, or toxins whatever their origin or method of production, of types and in quantities that have no justification for prophylactic, protective or other peaceful purposes;
2. Weapons, equipment or means of delivery designed to use such agents or toxins for hostile purposes or in armed conflict.

Chemical Weapons Convention (CWC) (signed 13–15 January 1993, and enters into force when 65 signatories have ratified the convention). This treaty took twenty-one years to negotiate and bans the development, production and stockpiling, and use of chemical weapons (CW) and requires their destruction. It complements and strengthens the 1925 protocol, which bans the use of CW in war (but not their possession), and the 1972 convention, which bans the development, production and stockpiling of biological and toxin weapons (but not poison gases). It fulfils the undertaking of states parties, under Article IX of the 1972 convention, to continue negotiations in good faith for 'early' agreement on chemical disarmament.

Article 1: General Obligations

5. Each State Party undertakes not to use riot control agents as a method of warfare.

Convention on The Prohibition of Military or Any Other Hostile Use of Environmental Modification Techniques (signed at Geneva on 18 May 1977). This convention looked forward to future developments in the field of modification of the environment whose use in warfare could have extremely harmful effects on human welfare. Parties to the convention undertook not to engage in military or hostile use of environmental modification techniques (this meant any technique for changing – through the deliberate manipulation of natural processes – the dynamics, composition, or structure of the earth, including its biota, lithosphere, hydrosphere and atmosphere, or of outer space) having widespread, long-lasting or severe effects as the means of destruction, damage or injury to any other state party. Definitions added to this convention for clarification were:

- 'widespread' – encompassing an area of several hundred square kilometres;
- 'long-lasting' – lasting for a period of months, or about a season;
- 'severe' – involving serious or significant disruption or harm to human life, natural and economic resources or other assets;
- 'modification techniques' – would effect, for example, earthquakes, changes in weather patterns, changes in climate patterns, changes in the ocean currents, changes in ozone layer and the state of the ionosphere.

Under the auspices of the United Nations, a *Convention on Prohibition or Restrictions on the Use of Certain Conventional Weapons which May Be Deemed to Be Excessively Injurious or to Have Indiscriminate Effects* (also known as the UN Inhumane Weapons Convention – UNWC) was agreed in Geneva in October 1980, and entered into force December 1983. This convention has no application to chemical, biological or nuclear weapons, but is targeted specifically at a category of weapons that may be thought to be 'inhumane' or 'dubious' (Kalshoven, 1987, p. 147). The term 'dubious' was coined because either the weapons themselves or the manner in which they are used are deemed not to be in accordance with the principles of the humanitarian law of armed conflict. The UNWC is what is known as an 'umbrella' treaty under which specific agreements can be integrated in the form of protocols. The convention, which does not apply to 'non-international' conflicts or civil wars, had 52 signatory states by June 1995, and 49 other states had ratified it. It was hoped that the UNWC would build on the 1977 Additional Protocols of the Geneva Conventions particularly with reference to Articles 35 and Article 36 which stated:

Article 35

1. In any armed conflict, the right of the Parties to the conflict to choose methods or means of warfare is not unlimited.
2. It is prohibited to employ weapons, projectiles and material and methods of warfare of a nature to cause superfluous injury or unnecessary suffering.
3. It is prohibited to employ methods or means of warfare which are intended, or may be expected, to cause widespread, long-term and severe damage to the natural environment.

Article 36

In the study, development, acquisition or adoption of a new weapon, means or method of warfare, a High Contracting Party is under an obligation to determine whether its employment would, in some or all circumstances, be prohibited by this Protocol or by any other rule of international law applicable to the High Contracting Party.

The substance of the UNWC is to be found in its annexed protocols namely:

- *Protocol 1*: Prohibition of use of non-detectable fragments.
- *Protocol 2*: Prohibitions or Restriction on the Use of Mines, Booby Traps and Other Devices.
- *Protocol 3*: Prohibitions or Restrictions on the Use of Incendiary Weapons.

The UNWC had no provisions for supervision or implementation, or for dealing with alleged violations, which severely limited its effectiveness. Nevertheless the UNWC was considered an achievement because it did refer to specific weapons and because it appeared to strike a balance between humanitarian imperatives and military considerations (Goldblat, 1995, p. 828). A UNWC Review Conference was held in Vienna between 25 September and 13 October 1995, and the results of this conference will be looked at a little more closely below.

To illustrate the issues surrounding the ethical, legal and control problems posed by NLWs, we will select several categories of NLWs and examine how they relate to international law and conventions. We will also look at some of the actions taken by the International Committee of the Red Cross (ICRC), NGOs and other elements of the international community to control and ban their deployment.

International Control and Prohibition of Non-Lethal Weapons: Case Studies

Blinding laser weapons

There is an extensive and specialized literature describing lasers and laser weapons, but excellent introductory reading relating to this section can be found in Doswald-Beck (ed.), 1993; ICRC, 1994; and Human Rights Watch Arms Project, 1995a and 1995b. Early stimulus for a ban on blinding laser weapons came when the governments of Sweden and Switzerland raised the subject at the 1986 International Conference of the Red Cross and at the UN General Assembly in 1987. The ICRC, noting the need to 'pay attention to new weapons developments to make sure the use of projected weapons would not violate international humanitarian law as codified in Article 36 of the 1977 First Additional Protocol to the 1949 Geneva Convention', arranged a meeting of consultant experts to examine blinding laser weapons. Between June 1989 and April 1991 a series of meetings was held which resulted in a comprehensive report *Blinding Weapons: Reports of the Meetings of Experts Convened by the International Committee of the Red Cross on Battlefield Laser Weapons 1989–1991* (Doswald-Beck (ed.), 1993). The report concluded that unless urgent action was taken, such weapons (which would be small and light, requiring only portable battery packs as their source of energy), would be readily available not only as weapons for soldiers, but also for use by terrorists and criminals. Several countries were already in a position to deploy and market such weapons. The ICRC, along with others, argued that anti-personnel blinding lasers posed a threat to civilians and soldiers alike, that they would cause unnecessary suffering and superfluous injury, and that these particularly cruel weapons should be outlawed. A focus for lobbying by the ICRC, some governments and NGOs such as the Human Rights Watch Arms Project, was the UNWC Review Conference set for September 1995. Opponents of laser weapons were not pleading for a ban on all lasers, but only on those that caused blindness. Lasers deployed as rangefinders or as purely anti-material or anti-sensor devices would not be affected by the proposed prohibition. It was realized that it was difficult to differentiate between intentional and accidental blinding during a battle, but this does not diminish the need or value of an international norm against blinding.[1] Supporters of battlefield lasers claim that they are more accurate and not so indiscriminate as other weapons. Whilst it is true that lasers do allow more precision targeting, the ICRC points out that there is nothing inherent in laser weapons that ensures their discriminate use or renders civilians safe from their effects.[2] They note that because a beam from a rifle may be used to scan a battlefield or a group of civilians, anyone whose eyes are hit would be blinded, usually permanently. This potential for scanning makes indiscriminate use more likely and tempting than with conventional rifles.

Intensive lobbying by some governments, NGOs and individuals took place before the UNWC Review Conference. There was resistance at this time firstly from states that were involved in the R&D of such weapons and resented interference, and secondly because others needed persuading that these laser weapons were not in the realm of science fiction but actually ready for deployment.[3] The technological

---

Two Proposals for the 1995 UNWC Review Conference

ICRC: Blinding as a method of warfare is prohibited. Laser weapons may not be used against the eyesight of persons

Swedish Government: It is prohibited to use laser beams as an anti-personnel method of warfare, with the intention or expected result of seriously damaging the eyesight of persons.

---

and industrial bases had developed so that these laser weapons could be mass-produced, would be the same price as a conventional rifle and, because of the prolific arms trade, would become readily available on the open market. Research was also under way to find methods of protecting combatants from the danger of laser weapons that were primarily designed for use as anti-equipment weapons. If a person, specifically the equipment operator, gets in the way of the laser beam, then of course they may be blinded. Barry Fox reported in the *New Scientist* on one effort to tackle this problem.[4] Neodymium lasers are especially risky because the near-infrared wavelength at which they operate is invisible to the human eye, so victims do not blink. Fox described a British-patented idea which takes advantage of the fact that neodymium lasers can also emit light at double frequency, with a clearly visible wavelength of 530 nanometres. Before the laser emits a full-power beam of invisible radiation, it sends out a warning burst of visible light. The warning shot ramps up from zero to maximum power in the space of a second. This is long enough for victims to blink or cover their eyes, but does not give them time to protect their electronic equipment.

Concerning blinding weapons, US government policy had argued that it was 'better to be blind than dead'. At this time the argument ran that blinding was a consequence not only associated with lasers, but also with other hazards encountered on battlefields, such as bullets and shrapnel, and all forms of battlefield blinding should be treated in the same way. Prior to the UNWC Review Conference, many US senators and congressmen expressed their support for a ban on blinding laser weapons, and on 31 July 1995 forty-eight members of the US Congress signed a letter to Secretary of Defense William Perry to this effect. They also wrote of the danger that the proliferation of such weapons could pose a potent threat to US troops: 'We dread the day when hundreds or thousands of American service men and women return home from combat to face the rest of their lives without eyesight. The development and spread of these weapons could also lead to widespread abuse against civilians by common criminals and terrorists.' On 1 September 1995 the US DoD announced a new policy on blinding lasers which stated that the DoD prohibited the use of lasers specifically designed to cause permanent blindness of unenhanced vision, and supported negotiations prohibiting the use of such weapons.[5] The DoD also withdrew its opposition to regulation of these weapons. The DoD press release stated in part:

> laser systems are absolutely vital to our modern military. Among other things, they are currently used for detection, targeting, range-finding, communications and target destruction. They provide a critical technological edge to US forces and allow our forces to fight, win and survive on an increasingly lethal battlefield. In addition, lasers provide significant humanitarian benefits. They allow weapons systems to be increasingly discriminate, thereby reducing collateral damage to civilian lives and property.

Groups such as Human Rights Watch, whilst welcoming this new policy, pointed out that the policy fell short of a ban on tactical laser weapons being used against the eyesight of individuals and thus allowed certain lasers that could blind to 'fall through the cracks'.[6] The US DoD does claim to have effective mechanisms in place to screen new weapons legally to ensure that their intended use is consistent with US law-of-war obligations (Barry et al., 1994, p. 15). In response to concern and protest, the British government stated that it had also halted work on laser weapons (*Guardian*, 23 May 1995).

At the 1995 UNWC Review Conference which ended on 13 October, a new protocol was adopted.[7] Protocol IV which banned blinding laser weapons should be considered as a landmark event and particularly welcome in that it signalled a new willingness of states to use humanitarian law to pre-empt an unwanted development rather than react belatedly to horrors that have already occurred (Molander, 1995). As in the case of dum-dum bullets, outlawed under the St Petersburg Declaration, a weapon had been banned before it had been used on the battlefield. But as for any convention, there were problems. Excluded from Protocol IV, as mentioned above under US policy, were lasers that may blind as an incidental or collateral effect during legitimate military employment of laser systems. This category would include the use of lasers against optical equipment such as binoculars. Human Rights Watch also reported that during the review conference the US and the UK were outspoken opponents of an explicit ban on blinding as a method of warfare. More work is needed to expand the number of countries that have signed and ratified the convention,[8] and continued vigilance and effort is required to block efforts to exploit the above loopholes in the convention.

Non-lethal riot control agents

In the USA, whilst law enforcement agencies may use riot control agents against US citizens, Executive Order 11850 of 10 April 1975 forbids first use 'in war except in defensive military modes to save lives such as: ... situations in which civilians are used to mask or screen attacks ... or to protect convoys from civil disturbances, terrorists and paramilitary organisations...'[9] This ruling was prompted by the routine use of CS in Vietnam. So although the use of riot control gases is restricted in the conduct of warfare (where it is feared that they could mask the use of more lethal agents), they can be used by the military in situations such as peacekeeping and anti-terrorist missions, and in controlling rioting prisoners of war in rear-echelon areas. The terminology of the Chemical Weapons Convention includes allowance for anti-personnel non-lethal chemical agents to be used for 'law enforcement including domestic riot control purposes'. As Perry Robinson comments (in ICRC, 1994, p. 94), unfortunately the convention does not define what it means by 'law enforcement' (whose law? what law? enforcement where? by whom?), though it does define what it means by 'riot control agent', namely 'any chemical ... which can produce rapidly in humans sensory irritation or disabling physical effects which disappear within a short time of exposure'. This is close to the definition of how a gas NLW would be used. If CS can be used in peacekeeping missions and for defensive military purposes there is a danger of blurring their operational utility, especially by military forces not well versed in the details of international conventions. Finally on this point, the CWC asks states not to use riot control agents as a 'method of warfare' without defining what is meant. Calmative agents, or sleep agents, have been proposed by some agencies for use as battlefield or riot control agents and there were reports that such agents were used by the Soviet army in Afghanistan. These reports claimed that affected mujaheddin would lie down and sleep until they woke in Soviet custody. These reports were disbelieved because such chemicals have proven ineffective (Cook et al., 1995, p. 83). In 1995 there were reports that the Tamil Tigers[10] used shells filled with CS gas against attacking Sri

Lankan army forces during their assault on the Tamil stronghold of Jaffna.[11] Rumours that the CS gas might be laced with a more lethal chemical agent caused some panic amongst troops, but no direct casualties were reported.

Acoustic Weapons

As we have seen, acoustic weapons have already been tested operationally by the British Army in Northern Ireland, and by the USA against General Noriega in Panama. To be effective, acoustic weapons must inflict some degree of pain and/or discomfort but, as for other weapons, consideration must be given as to whether their use: is discriminate or indiscriminate; is proportional to military necessity and humanity; and does not cause unnecessary suffering. Three main types of acoustic weapon are under development: high-intensity sound weapons, ultra-low-frequency (infrasound) weapons, and sonic bullets. During the development of acoustic weapons there have been problems with focusing the sound waves sufficiently, with the result that unacceptable collateral effect (that is, effect on civilians and noncombatants) has occurred. Used as a weapon in war, under accepted norms and conventions, it would be 'permissible' to deploy acoustic weapons to kill and seriously injure, provided their effects were within the caveats already discussed. But when used against civilians, for example in riot control, different considerations and guidelines must apply. It is vital that the danger of the blurring between civil and military uses of new weapons technology is explicitly acknowledged. Cook et al. (1995) report the development, by Russian researchers, of packets of sonic energy (sonic bullets) which can be accurately directed and propelled for hundreds of yards towards an enemy. The level of energy can be selected to be lethal or non-lethal. If this technique is refined and perfected, then a non-lethal weapon that is discriminate, proportionate to necessity, and does not cause unnecessary suffering will have been produced.

Threatening Citizens' Rights

In a report to the US National Science Foundation (Security Planning Corporation, 1972, pp. 39–43), objections to the introduction of NLWs in the context of the social consequences of improving the coercive technology available to law enforcement officials were raised. The report listed four areas of concern:

1. Law enforcement officers would be more vindictive if armed with NLWs and less accountable than when armed with lethal firepower. The example is given in the report of one police chief who refused to issue chemical aerosol sprays to his men because he felt they would use them to 'torture' people, and his department would be unable to keep tabs on what was happening.
2. NLWs may violate community norms.
3. The development and utilization of NLWs is a sign of repression. This view was supported by the British Society for Social Responsibility in Science, which wrote thus of new non-lethal technologies being employed in Northern Ireland: 'The timing of the introduction of new weapons suggests that their use is dictated less by the immediate requirements of riot control, than by the wish to discourage people even from exercising their democratic rights of peaceful demonstration.'[12] In the USA there was a feeling that NLWs would be primarily used against dissident minorities.
4. NLW development emphasizes symptoms rather than underlying causes of crime and political protest. The report quotes Hans Mattick of the University of Chicago Law School: 'Rubber bullets and shields do no good. We need human resources and change, not gimmicks. It's so much more important that men in crises not deprive each other of their humanity.'

Non-Lethal Weapons and Torture

The UK Channel 4 *Dispatches* TV programme 'The Torture Trail' alleged that some British firms (including Royal Ordnance, which is owned by British Aerospace) were prepared to supply electric-shock batons made in Germany for export to the Middle East. These batons can be used as instruments of torture. A disturbing report in the *Guardian* (12 August 1995) read:

> The Federation of American Scientists (FAS) discovered that between 1991 and 1993 14 licences valued at $5 million were issued for exports to Saudi Arabia under Department of Commerce category OA84C, covering 'saps, thumbcuffs, thumbscrews, leg irons, shackles and handcuffs; specially designed instruments of torture; straight jackets, plastic handcuffs'. A further 14 licences valued at $5.4 million were allowed for a category including 'stun guns, shock batons, electric cattle prods'.

Electric stun guns in these export batches included types such as the Taser, which delivers a high-voltage shock. Despite the manufacturer's assertion that this weapon is non-lethal, research in the USA claimed that the Taser had contributed to at least nine deaths.[13] At least one British Aerospace executive was disciplined for attempting to sell Taser guns to reporters posing as arms buyers, but he was soon back in full employment by the company at defence equipment exhibitions (*Guardian*, 6 September 1995).

Conclusion

For some people the concept that there can be methods of killing or injuring in a war that are more acceptable than others is anathema. Others point to international conventions that have had real influence and success in stigmatizing and controlling particularly obscene weapons. The examples of dum-dum bullets and poison gas immediately come to mind. The principle of 'unnecessary suffering' does not prohibit weapons that cause extreme suffering or extensive injuries, but only those that cause unnecessary suffering or superfluous injuries. The 'unnecessary suffering' principle directs that a balance should be struck between the military advantage that the use of a particular weapon may be expected to achieve and the degree of injury and suffering that it is likely to cause. Military and law enforcement commanders must be careful in choosing the weapons they deploy in order to carry out a particular operation. Weapons classified under the term 'non-lethal' extend the range of options open to policy makers and field commanders. As we have already seen, for those working in the fields of arms control and humanitarian law, a range of definitional and terminological problems surrounds NLWs. What should be a common purpose is a determination to reduce suffering and fatalities for those caught up in the brutality of warfare.

> The questions at issue in humanitarian law, no matter how varied and complicated, can be reduced to two fundamental problems: viz., the problem of balancing humanity against military necessity, and the obstacles posed by the sovereignty of states. (Kalshoven, 1987, p. 159)

As Goldblat reminds us, the rules of conduct set in time of peace for belligerents may not withstand the pressure of military expedience generated during the course of hostilities (Goldblat, 1995, p. 835). But he also concludes that there is an intrinsic link between humanitarian law and disarmament.

> This link was recognized by the signatories to the CW Convention when in the preamble they expressed the belief that positive results achieved in prohibiting or restricting the use of certain conventional weapons would facilitate talks on disarmament with a view to halting the production, stockpiling and proliferation of these weapons. (Goldblat, 1995, p. 835)

With rapid technological advances making a new generation of NLWs available to police and military forces, and with the blurring of military and police 'missions', states must stop being satisfied with tinkering with the language of existing treaties and conventions and instead must negotiate new documents. These must include weapons that until a few years ago were regarded as being in the realms of science fiction, and they must also make provision for weapons that are now on the drawing board. For example, some of the new antimaterial supercaustics we have referred to earlier may be corrosive and toxic enough to kill or injure people, and thus should be banned under the terms of the CWC. New conventions should also take into account the types of peacekeeping and peace-enforcing missions that military forces are increasingly being asked to perform; missions that inevitably involve closer contact with civilians and humanitarian considerations. Some critics of the CWC, which bans the use of chemical riot control agents against combatants in wartime, say it would be a tragic irony if nations used lethal means against non-combatants because non-lethal means were banned by international convention (Council for Foreign Relations, 1995, p. 12).

The role of pressure and campaigning groups, such as the ICRC and Human Rights Watch Arms Project, is vital in publicizing and informing the public about new weapons systems and the need for their regulation and, when possible, their prohibition. Mobilization of the public conscience puts pressure on governments to do something about inhumane weapons. The scientific community could do more to remind colleagues of their ethical responsibilities: blinding lasers were developed in laboratories by people in white coats[14] who must in some way be held accountable. To many it seems incredible that there is still a demand by some to find yet more ways of killing and maiming fellow human beings.

The overriding goal should be to prevent or banish war completely, and to achieve complete disarmament. But this is a utopian dream. In face of this reality, any measures that help to control, regulate or ban particular weapons and that attempt to make war fighting more 'humane' and discriminate must be applauded.

Notes

1. ICRC (1995) *Blinding Laser Weapons: Questions and Answers*.
2. *Ibid.*
3. There was evidence that laser weapons were already being marketed. For example the Chinese company China North Industries Corp. (Norinco) was advertising its ZM-87 Portable Laser Disturber which as well as damaging or invalidating enemy photo-electric sensors was designed also to 'injure or dizzy the eyes' up to a range of 3km. With the addition of a 7x sighting telescope, the effective distance of human eye injury could be increased to 5km. Comparable devices had been developed by French, Russian, UK and US armed forces since at least the early 1980s (*International Defense Review*, May 1995). In May 1995, Human Rights Watch Arms Project issued a report that identified ten US blinding laser weapons.
4. Barry Fox, 'Don't look now', *New Scientist*, 24 June 1995.
5. News release, Office of Assistant Secretary of Defense (Public Affairs), Washington, DC, 1 September 1995. Ref No: 482–95.
6. The Human Rights Watch Arms Project specifically mentioned the Laser Countermeasure System (LCMS) which is deployed as an anti-sensor or anti-optical system. However, when used against an individual employing an optical device, the LCMS would not destroy the optic, but rather would blind the individual as the optic magnifies the laser beam and focuses it on the most sensitive part of the eye. The USA may claim that the LCMS and similar systems are 'specifically designed to cause permanent blindness of unenhanced vision' but the reality is they are likely to blind those using optical instruments (Human Rights Watch Arms Project, news release, 6 September 1995). In fact the USA did terminate the LCMS programme in October 1995, whilst retaining other anti-optical weapons.
7. Because there was so much unfinished business, especially concerning the failure to negotiate a strengthened Protocol II concerning prohibitions and restrictions on the use of land mines, two further sessions were scheduled for January and April 1996.
8. It requires twenty signatures to ratify the protocol for it to come into force.
9. Quoted in Collins (1995), p. 5.
10. The Tamil Tigers were fighting for an independent Tamil homeland – Tamil Eelam – in the north and east of Sri Lanka.
11. *Agence France-Press International News*, 26 November 1995.
12. Quoted in J. Rosenhead and P. Smith, 'Ulster Riot Control: A Warning', *New Scientist*, 12 August 1971, p. 374.
13. Report by Trench B. Allen in *US Journal of Forensic Sciences*. Quoted in Pallister (1995a).
14. *Lancet*, Editorial, 17 December 1994.

5

Strategic Implications into the Twenty-first Century: The Concept of Benign Intervention

We will now look to the implications for the future development and use of non-lethal weapons within the framework of local and global security needs, particularly in the area known as 'humanitarian intervention'. If present trends continue, existing states will continue to fracture, with corresponding regional insecurity and violence; weak states will undergo internal divisions and conflict; and there will be a growth in ruthless regimes and dedicated terrorist gangs or liberation movements, with access to sophisticated weapons and technology bases, whose values regarding human rights and the worth of human life will be widely different. Scenarios for future conflict include: clashes of cultures (and perhaps civilizations); border disputes; struggles for vital natural resources such as water, good agricultural land, food, oil and other marine sources; migration of people because of poverty and starvation. Failed states will demand attention from the international community for humanitarian peacekeeping and peace enforcement operations. The list goes on. Policy makers in some states must consider public opinion regarding civilian and noncombatant casualties during such interventions. These concerns will have to be built into operational plans and guidelines, with more constraints and accountability for military forces, and clearer analysis and consideration given to the question of appropriate levels of response to national and international security threats.

Military intervention forces can be put into four broad categories: national military forces; coalition military forces; forces acting under the auspices of the UN and regional security organizations; and forces of national liberation. We have outlined the general doctrinal and operational requirements of these and the possible utility of NLWs in the preceding chapters. In this chapter we want to discuss a further category of military intervention force, which would operate within an overall philosophy called Benign Intervention (BI). The doctrine and operational deployment of NLWs are seen as integral to this military force, which for our purposes we will conceive of as an independent United Nations Benign Intervention Force (UNBIF). The spectrum of operations of such a force could be broad, including conflict prevention (for example, deployment of its personnel as monitors or observers in areas of tension), peace enforcement, and wider peacekeeping (see Table 5.2, p. 116).

This chapter is somewhat speculative, and the concept of a Benign Intervention Force is not here postulated as a proposal, more as a vehicle to explore the controversies surrounding humanitarian intervention and the ways in which NLWs could be integrated ethically into humanitarian intervention forces. The very question of a force such as UNBIF raises fundamental questions about issues such as collective international security, the right of intervention and non-intervention under the humanitarian banner, the criteria and principles that inform humanitarian intervention, the debate about the militarization of humanitarian intervention, and the ethics of using force in such situations. These are concerns with far-reaching implications because nations and groups have widely varying ideas about what constitutes a global vision for the future, and about 'how the world should be', and the role of any world peace and law enforcement agencies. In this chapter we will broadly consider these questions within the context of Benign Intervention.

An Independent UN Force?

It is appropriate first to review briefly the history behind the idea of a global force, and the political and military problems that have dogged it. The idea of an independent international force capable of intervening to stop or prevent violent international conflict is not new. Weber, in an article 'The Evolution of Plans for an International Military Force for Peace' (Weber, 1995), reviewed attempts at creating such a force from the time of the ancient Greeks up to the proposals outlined by Boutros Boutros-Ghali in *An Agenda For Peace* (Boutros-Ghali, 1992). These included William Penn's famous essay in 1693 *Towards the Present and Future Peace of Europe*, the attempts by the League of Nations after the First World War to set up a permanent army of the League, and the various propositions suggested under the aegis of the United Nations since 1945. In 1960 the Federal Union (Federal Union, 1960) considered an armed force which would build on the experience and structure of the United Nations Emergency Force (UNEF) sent to Egypt in 1956. The Federal Union proposed a force that could operate in three main roles: (1) as a Light Force, with up to 20,000 men and unable to undertake offensive operations; (2) as a Medium Force, with enough strength in military operations so long as not directed against a great power; (3) as a Heavy Force which would enable the UN to be the effective policeman of the world. Of the three roles, the idea of a Light Force attracted most support. Waskow (1967) outlined the requirements for a special transnational Peacekeepers Academy under UN auspices to train men and women for

> a new profession of peacekeeping that would both deal with crises of out-right violence that threatened world peace, and, between crises, deal with some of the chronic underlying problems that lead to violence. (Waskow, 1967, p. 7)

Waskow's proposal for a first step toward a United Nations Transnational Peacekeeping Force suggested that the initiators of the Peacekeepers Academy should be private organizations because they were less constrained than the UN and could get the project off the ground more quickly. Brian Urquhart (1991) described two types of UN military operation: traditional peacekeeping and large-scale collective enforcement. Peacekeeping forces are deployed after a ceasefire has been agreed and may use weapons only in self-defence, whilst enforcement actions allow for the aggressive use of lethal force. Urquhart argued the need for a third category of international military operation lying somewhere between peacekeeping and large-scale enforcement. This third force would be relatively small and its interventions would essentially be armed police actions intended to 'put an end to random violence and to provide a reasonable degree of peace and order so that humanitarian relief work could go forward and a conciliation process could commence'.

Proposals for some sort of permanent 'world army' have always been viewed with scepticism. The UN Charter, Article 2.7, excludes intervention into the internal affairs of member states unless international security is threatened (Article 39), but on a few occasions the UN has initiated or supported enforcement actions, as was the case for Korea (1951), Kuwait (1991), Somalia (1991), and Bosnia (1995). Fears have been expressed of creating an international force which may become uncontrollable and a threat to national sovereignty. Other unresolved foundational problems for such a force include:

- Who would pay for a UN force?
- What would be the policy for recruitment – should the force be independently recruited, or allocated troops from member countries?
- Would it be possible to create an *esprit de corps*? What would be the common language of the force?
- Who would have overall military command? Individual national army commanders are unwilling to relinquish final control of their allocated forces.
- What would be the policy for equipping the force? What type of weapons would be needed, and where would they be acquired? There would be problems of nations being unwilling to share classified technologies and weapons systems freely.
- Where would such a force be based?
- To whom would it be accountable? For example, UN forces are not direct signatories to any of the international weapons conventions or to international humanitarian law, and some commentators think that the political structure of the UN is incapable of managing and controlling such a force.
- How would the force be trained? What skills (military and non-military) are thought to be necessary? There could be tension between traditional army discipline, values and operational methods and the new concepts required for a UN military force.

Many of these questions are tackled by Conetta and Knight (1995) in their study *Vital Force: A Proposal for the Overhaul of the UN Peace Operations System and for the Creation of a UN Legion*, where they put forward detailed proposals for a UN peace operations legion within a framework of UN reforms. These include: the formation of a Military Advisory and Co-operation Council as an adjunct to the Security Council; the formation of a multinational Field Communication and Liaison Corps to serve as a modular command, control, and communication framework for multinational operations; the development of a staff structure in the UN Secretariat that can plan and manage joint and combined efforts across the full spectrum of peace operations; and the formation and development of a permanent UN standing force comprising four brigades and a field support structure (a total of 43,750 personnel) to complement and augment member-state contributions to peace operations. Conetta and Knight estimated the cost of maintaining such a UN peace operations legion to be US$2.6 billion annually. In 1995 a 34-member UN special committee reported that a standing army would give an 'undesirable military image' to an organization dedicated to world peace.[1] Committee members also objected that the use of a UN army in internal conflicts would be unacceptable and would erode the principle of state sovereignty, and that such an army would give the UN Secretary-General too wide a military authority. The USA was opposed to the creation of such an army. In *An Agenda for Peace* (1992), Boutros Boutrous-Ghali, the Secretary-General, had recommended to the UN Security Council

> the utilization of peace-enforcement units in clearly defined circumstances and with their terms of reference specified in advance. Such units from member states would be available on call and would consist of troops that have volunteered for such service. They would have to be more heavily armed than peacekeeping forces and would need to undergo extensive preparatory training within their national forces. Deployment and operation of such forces would be under the authorization of the Security Council and would, as in the case of peacekeeping forces, be under the command of the Secretary-General. (Boutrous-Ghali, 1992, p. 26)

It is not surprising that this proposal was unpopular with UN members who were not included in the Security Council decision-making processes, since it highlighted again what some perceived as the undemocratic nature of the UN. An idea from Boutros-Ghali that received more support was that nations should commit themselves to the provision of 'earmarked capabilities' (Eberle, 1993) or 'standby forces' which were not to be used for peace enforcement actions but for peacekeeping operations. They were intended to be able to be rapidly deployed in a preventive mode, and by March 1994 some twenty-three countries had pledged troops for this purpose.[2] But as Bennis notes, 'when the call came to make those troops available for the real here-and-now UN peacekeeping commitment in war-torn Rwanda, every single one of the 23 countries refused' (Bennis, 1994, p. 173).

The question of such a standing UN force must be considered within the context of general reform within the UN, and in the context of the peacemaking and peacekeeping roles it has developed. It must be remembered that peacekeeping is not actually described in the

UN Charter, though articles 39 and 42 allow for the use of both political and military intervention (forcible and non-forcible) in peace and security operations.[3] Article 51 is also useful for justifying intervention under 'the right of collective self-defence'. In 1992 the UN General Assembly passed a resolution calling for the reform of the Security Council so that it was expanded to include more permanent (especially Germany and Japan) and non-permanent members, which would reflect the growth in the UN's membership since its inception. The Security Council, which has 15 members out of a total UN membership of 180, was seen by many as undemocratic and unrepresentative and weighted to 'northern power' bases. Thus decisions as to how, when, or if to deploy UN peacekeeping forces were not arrived at democratically, with wide consultation amongst the body of the UN membership, who were meant to be 'equal states' within the UN framework.

Some military analysts in the USA have argued that it is not beneficial for US forces to participate in peacekeeping duties because it impairs their readiness for war fighting, which is their primary function. After a peacekeeping mission soldiers have to undergo extensive retraining to regain the standard of operational combat proficiency they were at before the outset of the peacekeeping duty (Roos, 1993, p. 17). Perhaps it would be more appropriate for the USA to avoid peacekeeping missions for its troops, and limit its actions to enforcement operations (Clarke, 1995, p. 34). A standing UN force could be specifically trained and equipped for a peacekeeping role which, in any case, it has been argued is not appropriate for assault and combat troops.

Before moving on to examine Benign Intervention more specifically, it is necessary to review two key debates that inform the very question of humanitarian intervention. These questions concern what criteria and principles should guide interventions, and the uneasiness of some observers that humanitarian intervention is becoming dangerously militarized and politicized.

Criteria and Principles for Humanitarian Intervention

There has been much debate about what constitute legitimate reasons for humanitarian intervention, both military and non-military, by the international community into a conflict situation (Lewer and Ramsbotham, 1993; Ramsbotham and Woodhouse, 1996). Most would agree that there must be a serious abuse or denial of fundamental human rights as defined in the UN Universal Declaration of Human Rights, or that a state must have failed, with no form of 'government' left to maintain law and order and to protect the population from genocide and, for example, molestation by warlords and bandits. There have been many attempts to draw up operating codes of conduct, criteria and framework principles to guide humanitarian intervention, and there is now an extensive literature covering this field. It is appropriate to review a sample of these attempts because a UNBIF-type force must operate from a baseline ethical framework that is, as near as possible, universally acceptable.

Meyer (1987, pp. 490–91) proposes as the main requirements for acceptable humanitarian intervention:

- existence of a real need for it (this deters unwelcome or unnecessary interference in a country's internal affairs)
- that its motive be humanitarian (where a humanitarian activity is 'concerned with human beings as such, and must not be affected by any political or military consideration')
- that it be the result of impartial consideration and no adverse distinction (distribution of assistance based as far as possible on actual need and not influenced by factors such as nationality, race, religion, social status, politics, positions of power etc.)
- official authorization
- adherence to governing agreements with the authorities concerned (these would relate to respect for the law of the host country, respect for agreed operational strategies etc.).

Weiss and Wiseman (1990, pp. 124–5) framed some recommendations or moral imperatives for humanitarian organizations and peacekeepers which included:

- They should be careful not to challenge or undermine the local culture.
- They should adopt a balanced relationship with the parties so as not to jeopardize their own legitimacy.
- They should make use of available, or help create indigenous, societal or other infrastructures for the management of aid.

Scheffer (Scheffer and Gardner, 1992) considered that the right of non-forcible humanitarian intervention by international aid agencies might arise when the following criteria are met:

- A manmade or natural disaster places large numbers of people at risk of losing their lives owing to a scarcity of adequate food or shelter, or an act of internal aggression leads to mass casualties among the civilian population. The commencement of refugee migrations would constitute prima facie evidence of such events.
- The local government cannot or will not meet the humanitarian needs arising from the disaster or act of internal aggression.
- The local government does not seek to prevent forcibly, and therefore acquiesces in, non-forcible intervention on its territory.
- The Security Council authorizes the intervention, perhaps insisting that the local government permit such an action and, where appropriate, co-operate with UN officials in the distribution of aid. Lightly armed UN guards should be regarded as justifiable participants in a non-forcible humanitarian intervention, to provide minimal security for aid personnel.

The American Refugee Committee (D. Weissbrodt, quoted in Cobey et al., 1993) suggested the following criteria should determine UN action:

- the number of persons affected by the humanitarian emergency
- the immediacy and severity of the threat to life
- the number of refugees or displaced persons who have been forced to flee
- a pattern of significant human rights abuses
- the inability or unwillingness of the government to cope with the crisis.

Minnear and Weiss (1995, pp. 57–103) drew up eight guiding principles for humanitarian action (also known as the Providence Principles):

- Relieving life-threatening suffering.
- Proportionality to need.
- Non-partisanship: the intervention is based on human need and suffering and not determined by other agenda, such as to acquire political and religious advantage.
- Independence: humanitarian intervenors should be able to respond without interference.
- Accountability.
- Appropriateness: the intervention should be tailored to local circumstances, enhancing rather than supplanting local resources.
- Understanding the context.

- Keeping sovereignty in its proper place: when sovereignty and relief of suffering clash, the latter should prevail.

The International Committee of the Red Cross (ICRC) has Seven Fundamental Principles for Humanitarian Intervention :

- Humanity: the purpose of the ICRC is to protect life and health, to prevent and alleviate human suffering, and to ensure respect for the human being.
- Impartiality: the ICRC makes no discrimination as to nationality, race, religious beliefs, class or political opinions. It endeavours to relieve the suffering of individuals, being guided solely by their needs, and to give priority to the most urgent cases of distress.
- Neutrality: the ICRC does not take sides in hostilities or engage at any time in controversies of a political, racial, religious or ideological nature.
- Independence.
- Voluntary service: the ICRC is not prompted in any manner by desire for gain.
- Unity: there can only be one Red Cross Society in any one country.
- Universality.

The deployment of a UN Benign Intervention Force (UNBIF) as a third-party intervenor must rest on a firm humanitarian base, within the parameters of described criteria and principles. The root problem for such intervenors is how to act non-politically in what is usually an intensely political arena. It will remain extremely difficult, whilst acting in the name of humanity, to transcend partisan politics in highly charged contexts where every action may be perceived as partisan.

Militarization and Politicization of Humanitarian Aid in Conflict Situations

NGOs and other agencies have worked for many years in dangerous and violent places, often arranging their security and protection from within the conflict area by negotiating with local militia and guerrillas. More recently the use of external forces, such as UN military units, has become more commonplace. These external UN interventions have often been authorized to cover and protect relief work, but not to protect the civilian populations. This has led to misunderstanding and resentment among local populations. For many this reliance on external forces is a dangerous trend:

> The militarization involved in having operations protected by external forces is a death-trap and will destroy all humanitarian activity by allowing it to become submerged in a politico-military context in which it cannot survive. (Rufin, 1993, p. 123)

Particularly as a result of war experiences in Bosnia, Iraq, Kurdistan, Somalia and Rwanda in the early 1990s, the issue of whether military force should be used to protect aid work became acute. Aid agency personnel had been deliberately targeted in many of the world's conflicts and were in need of some sort of protection. Policy at the UN changed with the passing of resolutions such as Resolution 770 which provided UN military protection for humanitarian convoys in Bosnia, and Resolution 794 which authorized UN troops to use 'all necessary means' in Somalia to secure the unimpeded distribution of aid. Later resolutions regarding Bosnia authorized the use of air strikes by NATO in support of humanitarian relief work (Pallister, 1994). In Rwanda, by May 1994 the situation had become so acute that even the ICRC abandoned its neutral stance and called for military intervention. The ICRC had thirteen volunteers slaughtered within a few days in Rwanda, and Oxfam called for intervention into Rwanda under the 1948 Genocide Convention.

The use of military forces to protect relief supplies and personnel is controversial, and in the 1990s became a topic of vigorous debate (UNHCR, 1993, p. 77). Dedring (1994) observes that soldiers trained for warfare and national security missions have little in common with relief personnel serving the goal of humanitarianism; he argues that tension between the two is likely. In Operation Restore Hope, an action supported by the UN, US troops landed in Somalia in December 1992 to provide military protection to humanitarian aid operations. This military intervention, whilst welcomed by UN agencies who blamed their operational difficulties on lack of protection from Somali warlords, was received with less enthusiasm by NGOs in the field (Stiefel, 1993, p. 16). US and later UN troops became involved in violent military confrontation with General Aideed and other warlords, thus making it more difficult for relief personnel to carry out their tasks. Since this experience, Dedring claims, the various partners in the UN system have become more wary of using soldiers in humanitarian operations (Dedring, 1994, p. 15). Operation Restore

Hope is an example of how the predominance of military and security aims over humanitarian aspects, and possibly even over humanitarian objectives, became so flagrant that for every dollar spent on humanitarian assistance, 10 dollars were spent on security operations. In fact the UN's 1993 budget for security operations equalled the total budget of the world food programme for the same year (Stiefel, 1993, p. 16).

Cornelio Sammarunga, of the ICRC, suggested that an overhaul of the international aid system was needed to impose a strict division between military intervention and humanitarian aid:

> There is an increasing blur between those two activities which is confusing our work and the work of other humanitarian bodies. (Luce, 1994)

This uneasiness over the encroaching activities of the military was also voiced by Médecins Sans Frontières (MSF), which asked, 'are we now experiencing armed charity?' (Jean (ed.), 1993, p. 111). MSF has legitimate cause for concern. During the 1991 US-led UN military intervention in Somalia, a building that MSF was using in Mogadishu was bombed by US troops in their hunt for Aideed, even though it was clearly marked with MSF flags and cars with red and white signs. Other humanitarian agencies, including the UN Development Programme and Action Internationale Contre le Faim, experienced similar problems (Boseley, 1993). What these military actions also revealed was the unaccountability of UN troops to international conventions. Since the UN is not itself a signatory to the Geneva Conventions, nobody appeared to take responsibility and MSF had to protest to the Security Council and to the UN commander in Somalia.

Not all military–civilian relationships have been so disharmonious. High degrees of international co-operation between military and civilian medical and relief teams have been demonstrated during some recent interventions into conflict situations (Miller and Kershaw, 1993; Sharp et al., 1994) and also in the emergency phase of natural disaster relief (Walker, 1992). In Operation Safe Haven, in northern Iraq in 1991, military personnel (from the US Air Force, British Royal Navy and Dutch Army medical units) and civilian agency intervention teams (International Rescue Service, AmeriCares, and UNICEF) co-operated to provide transport, food, measles vaccination, clean water and sanitation with prompt prevention and treatment of dehydration and infectious disease. It has been claimed that because of the military's expertise and training in command, control and communications the military is best suited to co-ordinate complex humanitarian operations. In Kurdistan in 1991, the US military was the *de facto* co-ordinating relief agency, and provided an organizational and commu-nications framework under which the fifteen other coalition forces, twenty relief organizations, and local Kurdish groups relocated almost half a million displaced persons during a two-week period (Sharpe et al., 1994). In some areas of northern Iraq, where there was no military presence, civilian agencies experienced difficulties with Iraqi armed forces who harassed them and forced them to leave their area of operation, abandoning millions of dollars' worth of equipment and supplies. Not all NGOs were happy with the military influence, how-ever, and some 'had a less helpful attitude and displayed indifference, if not open hostility to the military elements of Operation Safe Haven' (Miller, 1992). Some military elements are aware of their limitations in the area of humanitarian aid work and Sharp et al. (1994) in evaluating one aspect of military involvement in Kurdistan, that re-lating to medical assistance, made the following observations:

1. The primary focus of military medicine is to support combat operations, not to provide emergency humanitarian assistance. This focuses primarily on acute care for previously healthy young adults with combat trauma. Once emergency treatment has occurred, injured troops are evacuated.
2. Deployable military medical facilities have minimum quantities of the emergency medications or supplies recommended by the World Health Organization (WHO) for disaster-affected populations, such as oral rehydration salts, paediatric supplies, and some common antibiotics.
3. The military pays little attention to sustainable redevelopment. In the Kurdistan intervention, the local and experienced community physicians and nurses were given scant support to contribute to the relief effort. Dependency on the 'outsiders' can develop, and there is a vacuum left when the intervenors leave.
4. Military supplies are in some cases inappropriate. For example, field rations containing pork were given to Muslims during the Kurdistan operation.
5. Few military officers, at that time, received any training in humani-tarian assistance, and there is often also a lack of training in the language, customs, and medical practices of other populations.
6. Military commanders do not always understand the relief organ-izations and their missions and agendas. This contributes to con-fusion and controversy over command-and-control – military versus

civilian ways of working. In Somalia, non-military agencies were torn between the reliance (at one stage) on the military for security, and their mandate to be neutral parties.

The increasing trend towards politicization and militarization is a real cause for concern. As we have seen, the sheer size of some humanitarian operations being undertaken has required assistance from the military, especially with provision of logistics and transport. This question of military involvement in NGO humanitarian work raises two main dilemmas. Some NGOs reason that military involvement in such work compromises its stated non-political nature, raises the temperature in a crisis and may turn humanitarian facilities and staff into targets. Other organizations conclude that the urgent need for relief and the intractability of some of the antagonists leave no choice but to utilize UN or other military protection (UNHCR, 1993, p. 77). In some operations, UN humanitarian agencies have now come to rely on the military for the protection of land convoys, security at air and sea ports, and the provision of airlifts (such as in Bosnia, Cambodia, Somalia, Northern Iraq). For Stiefel (1993) the integration of humanitarian assistance into more military peacekeeping operations helps to justify the actual existence of some military elements which, since the end of the Cold War, are looking for new functions to help legitimize their existence.

The preceding section has introduced some of the main debates surrounding humanitarian intervention. Bearing these in mind, we will now look a little more closely at the concept of Benign Intervention.

Benign Intervention

Benign Intervention is conceptualized as a holistic philosophy that would include and integrate a role for non-lethal weapons in the military element of conflict intervention. The term 'benign' is chosen to indicate that the ethos of the intervention is humanitarian, benevolent (with the intention of stopping violence and bloodshed), and philanthropic for all conflicting parties. Benign Intervention consists of military and non-military components, and in the non-military component indigenous and international NGOs play a vital part. High priority is given to the following: acceptable principles and criteria for intervening; behaving in a manner that demonstrates as humane an approach as possible to peace enforcement (war fighting); showing concern for the victims; and a continual search for opportunities for non-violent conflict resolution.

Benign Intervention is much more than just a military operation to stop fighting (peace enforcement); it is in addition a process that includes conflict prevention, peacekeeping and peace building activities. Building on an initial concept proposed by Panvel (1994), a process consisting of four elements could be envisaged (see Table 5.2):

Element 1   Prevention: preventing the outbreak of violence.

Element 2   Benign Military Peace Enforcement: this would entail the deployment of a UN Benign Intervention Force for the purposes of: stopping the fighting, separating the combatants, and enforcing a ceasefire using 'benign military intervention'.

Element 3   Peacekeeping: humanitarian aid provision, demobilization and demilitarization, recovery and information gathering. Governance implementation.

Element 4   Peace building: building long-term economic, legal, security and cultural structures at community and national levels. Reconciliation.

These elements would inevitably overlap, and would need to be fully integrated and interlinked. Before the military intervention of Element 2 occurs, all efforts at peaceful settlement should have been attempted – indeed, the need to resort to military intervention should be viewed as a failure by the international community. There are many official and non-official channels for non-military intervention available which include: international diplomacy; UN 'good offices' – Chapter VI of the UN Charter, 'Pacific Settlement of Disputes', provides opportunities for the Security Council and General Assembly to attempt resolution, for example through mediation; regional security or co-operation organizations such as OSCE, OAU, OAS, ASEAN and SAARC may have a part to play; UN agencies and other inter-governmental and transnational organizations; non-governmental organizations and the International Committee of the Red Cross; eminent persons groups; non-official mediation, for example citizen diplomacy or two-track diplomacy.

One function of splitting Benign Intervention into these four elements is an attempt to separate out its military and non-military aspects. As we have seen, there has been much debate about the blurring of military and non-military phases of intervention, and about the politicization of humanitarian aid. This has caused confusion not

Table 5.1   Spectrum of Benign Intervention

Intervention	Prevention	Peace Enforcement	Peacekeeping	Peace Building
Type	Non-military Civilian/police	Military (UNBIF)	Non-military Civilian	Non-military Civilian

only with the 'targets' of the intervention, but also within the UN organizations:

> The UN's humanitarian organizations interact not only with each other but also with the political and military side of the United Nations. As the UN has become more active in what is now called peace enforcement, a widening cleavage has developed between UN organizations whose tasks are humanitarian and other parts of the UN operational apparatus whose preoccupation is for 'peace and security'. As a result, the UN is suffering a serious case of schizophrenia. (Minnear and Weiss, 1995)

We think it is important for everyone to be clear which culture (type) is prevalent at particular phases in an intervention, especially if it to be considered benign. Some would argue that any use of force (by this is meant the use of weapons) should not be termed 'benign' at all. But that is another debate. Simply, the relationship within the context of Benign Intervention is represented in Table 5.1. It is important, when attempting to rebuild a culture of peace, that the role of a military force (here within the concept of Benign Intervention) is recognized only for its specific enforcement role. Civilian structures must be built up as quickly as possible to provide the infrastructure and logistics for humanitarian aid delivery. Amongst other things, this helps to demilitarize the situation, but it also demonstrates that it is not only the military that has the expertise and resources to act efficiently and effectively. Civilians must regain ascendancy as soon as possible.

Element 1

Element 1 of Benign Intervention consists of a wide range of measures which can be implemented by outside intervenors with the objective of preventing a situation of tension and dispute becoming violent. A

Table 5.2   Benign Intervention

Element 1	Element 2	Element 3	Element 4
Prevention	Peace enforcement (UNBIF)	Peacekeeping	Peace building
Consent	No consent	Consent	Consent
Support role Policing role	Combat role	Policing role (Combat reserve)	Support role
Helping	Stopping Separating	Recovery Maintenance	Reconstruction Reconciliation
Short-term	Short-term	Medium-term	Long-term

Mediation
Economic aid
Community support
Fact-finding
Social development

       Protection of humanitarian aid
       Establishing communications
       Provision of shelter and security
       Mediation
       Negotiation

              War crimes tribunals
              Infrastructure reconstruction
              Humanitarian aid
              Refugee resettlement
              Political reconfiguration
              Demobilization and rehabilitation
              Early warning monitors

                    Therapy/reconciliation
                    Conflict prevention mechanisms
                    Conflict resolution mechanisms
                    Follow-up support
                    Peace education

                          Withdrawal

coalition of governments, NGOs, the ICRC, and intergovernmental and transnational agencies should work together in a complementary fashion to help create and strengthen forces for peace. Their activities should include mediation and negotiation, political and economic support, and perhaps community policing. Element-1-type interventions aim to create space and time for non-military conflict resolution initiatives to be fully explored.

Element 2

The second element of Benign Intervention is conceived as the impartial intervention of a military force trained and equipped to halt violent and armed conflict. Panvel originally proposed an intervention force equipped with non-lethal weapons, to signify that the fundamental purpose was not intentionally to injure or kill anybody, either combatants or non-combatants, and that the force intended the absolute minimum use of violence (Panvel, 1994, p. 3). The less violent the intervention, the fewer post-conflict problems such as reconstruction, injuries and revenge. Whilst military action is under way, negotiations must also be encouraged and facilitated – a twin-track approach. It is vital, once a decision to use military enforcement has been taken, that the operation is as early and as rapid as possible to break the spiral of violence before 'lock-in' occurs. The combatants engaged must believe that the military force intervening 'means business' and should be taken seriously, so from a military perspective they must be 'hit hard' to demonstrate such resolve. For many military analysts and strategists this means that a force must also be equipped with the usual range of conventional weapons, with the determination to use them if NLWs do not achieve the objective of stopping and separating the protagonists. It may be that the UN will subcontract more of the enforcement-type actions to military alliances (such as NATO), or even to national contingents that have units equipped and trained for aggressive combat roles.

An UNBIF may be authorized to intervene to:

- protect aid convoys to ensure the delivery of shelter, food and medicines;
- protect populations threatened with, or suffering from, gross human rights abuses or genocide;
- restore law and order when a state is no longer functioning;
- stop the fighting between, and separate, warring factions.

Many scenarios could face a military UN Benign Intervention Force, but one of the most difficult and potentially explosive is the handling of large crowds and riots. To help understand the tactical implications of the use of non-lethal riot control technologies, Stanton (1996) identified some key features for riot control which will have important implications for peacekeepers. Riots occur more frequently when there has been a breakdown in law and order and will usually involve large numbers of people (often entire communities) and will be more lethal. What looks like rioting in Third World countries, says Stanton, is in fact a form of warfare akin to low-level guerrilla warfare – and frequently the lethal intent of the rioters is directed towards the forces trying to restore order. Riots will be more carefully organized, and mixed in with the crowd will be three groups: a small number of armed fighters equipped with the usual array of lethal weapons; semi-armed rioters carrying clubs, bricks, knives and so on; and unarmed supporters who act as a screen around their armed colleagues. These three groups often operate under some type of chain of command. Riot organizers will quite deliberately employ women and children both as active rioters and as cover. Stanton states that this is because warlords and other faction leaders in Somalia, for example, understood US squeamishness at the possibility of harming women and children.

It is in situations like the rioting described above where non-lethal weapons technology is beginning to provide commanders with more options before having to resort to lethal force. When lethal force *is* resorted to, those who have come to protect in the name of 'humanity' come to be perceived as aggressors and oppressors rather than friends and allies.

The concept of Benign Intervention offers space to design a completely new type of military or police intervention force with the appropriate doctrine, policy and strategy relating especially to Benign Intervention Elements 2 and 3. Ideally soldiers should be recruited who have a genuine commitment to and understanding of peacemaking in the broader sense, as opposed to fighting for vested and national interests. Such soldiers should realize that in one respect the missions they will be asked to undertake will be more dangerous than 'traditional' war fighting. They will be expected to put greater emphasis on non-lethal means, which implies taking more risks before resorting to lethal force. This could well put their own lives in greater danger. There are several options for the structure of a military UN Benign Intervention Force:

1. a military force equipped only with non-lethal weapons
2. a military force equipped with non-lethal weapons and lethal weapons for self-defence only
3. a force consisting of two units: the first with non-lethal weapons only, the second held in close reserve and equipped with lethal weapons to be deployed if required
4. a force with fully integrated lethal (defensive and offensive) weapons and non-lethal weapons.

Whatever military structure is decided upon, before the force is deployed it is vital that a coherent political policy is formulated, that clear and transparent mandates and mission statements are agreed on, that realistic rules of engagement with some flexibility are provided, that the necessary logistic and support bases are established, and that the political and military command-and-communication channels are functioning and integrated.

An UN Benign Intervention Force equipped with lethal and non-lethal weapons must have rules of engagement that are clear and realistic. Lessons can be drawn from the experience of previous UN peacekeeping initiatives and these must be underpinned by the fundamental principle of using minimum force. Generally troops deployed in humanitarian support operations have been expected only to use heavy weapons in a reactive rather than prophylactic manner, and not to open fire to punish, interdict or anticipate hostile force activities (Mackinlay, 1994, p. 27). Berkowitz (1994) examined the rules of engagement, that is, the written orders that define what type of force troops can use, and when, for UNPROFOR in Bosnia. He points out that rules of engagement have a two-way function:

> First they are intended to make sure that military operations are consistent with policy objectives; civilian leaders can review ROE [rules of engagement] to determine if they are too violent, too risky, or result in too much collateral damage. Secondly ROE are intended to provide a clear set of guidelines for the commander and his troops, under the presumption that the military's role is to carry out orders and not make policy decisions. (Berkowitz, 1994, p. 635)

The rules of engagement for UNPROFOR were complex and used the 'option' or 'decision tree' approach, rather than the more simple and concise instructions demanded, for example, by US commanders. In Berkowitz's opinion the rules of engagement were too complicated and restrictive, and did not allow the UN forces to carry out dangerous missions effectively in hostile territory at an acceptable level of risk. More specific lessons regarding non-lethal weapons can be derived from the experience of US Marines in Somalia, where lethal and non-lethal weapons were classed together for the purposes of the rules of engagement. This meant that lethal weapons could only be used if a soldier's life was in imminent danger. It was later argued that what is needed are rules that reflect a 'seamless sliding scale of force options' which incorporate classifying weapons according to the degree of probability that they will cause death and according to the degree of provocation to use them (Becker and Heal, 1996, p. 64). Later in this chapter we will imagine a possible scenario for an UN Benign Intervention Force peace enforcement action.

Element 3

Whereas the role of a UN Benign Intervention Force in Element 2 was about peace enforcement, its role changes in Element 3 to that of peacekeeping. We move from a situation where consent of the belligerents was not required,[4] to a cessation of hostilities where consent and co-operation from all parties is required. But consent is something that a peacekeeper can expect to have bits of, from certain people, in certain places, for certain things and for certain periods of time (HMSO, 1995, pp. 2–6). Peace enforcement may create the conditions for peacekeeping; otherwise experience indicates that belligerents usually consent to third-party peacekeeping when they have fought themselves to exhaustion and their losses have become unacceptable, or they have achieved their objectives.

Element 3 requires a different type of deployment, a change from combat soldiers to personnel with expertise in 'peace keeping' in the non-military sense. If peacekeeping is about having consent, then there is no role now for combat troops, except perhaps to be held ready in reserve in case violence moves back into a war-fighting mode again. Non-lethal weapons may now have a lower-range function in this policing role. Element 3 peacekeepers would instigate training of local police forces, and in the initial stages would work alongside them. The sensitive job of arresting and identifying suspects who have committed alleged war crimes, and collating evidence must begin quickly. The peace enforcement and peacekeeping elements work to create 'humanitarian space' for UN agencies and NGOs to deliver humanitarian aid to refugees and local people without harassment. Demobilization and rehabilitation of fighters begins – in many instances there will be a problem in re-educating and socializing child soldiers.[5] Work begins on the long-term rebuilding of the political and civil infrastructure, including legal and health systems.

Element 4

Element 4 represents the long-term support from the international community, across a wide range of strategies, that is required to put a solid foundation in place for peace and stability. This may mean offering generous economic and trade relationships to help reach a stage where intervention and assistance from outside is no longer required. Early warning and conflict prevention mechanisms must be constructed, and non-violent social conflict management and conflict resolution schemes must be put in place. Disputes between groups that have the potential to flare into larger-scale violence could be referred to a UN regional conciliation and mediation commission.

It is possible now to construct a military intervention scenario which pulls together the various elements of non-lethality within the constraints and caveats of our preceding discussions. As we have seen, technology is providing a new range of non-lethal weapons, some of which are in active use today, and it is with this knowledge that we can speculate on or imagine a future intervention force using non-lethal weapons. This force might be part of an existing national army or regional military security grouping, or it could be the foundation of a future UN standing army. In the short to medium term, it will be the former, but for the sake of our discussion we imagine a future scenario using a UN Benign Intervention Force. Our own personal positions lie within the realm of demilitarizing the UN and for broader initiatives regarding disarmament and arms conversion, and the promotion of a civilian ethos to interventions. It is not our objective here to try and 'sanitize' war fighting or to give the impression that we think that wars will not remain bloody and violent affairs. But in the face of the reality that non-lethal weapons will become integrated in war-fighting and peace support operations, it is vital that we explore how they may be used. This type of exercise will open up the debate further with regard to benign and malign military aspects, and will also stimulate discussion of the broader ethical questions and implications concerning the use of force and non-force, of whatever kind, in outside intervention. In the simplistic scenario below, all the non-lethal weapons have been deployed in various situations or are in advanced development phases.

Scenario 2000 AD: UNBIF Peace Enforcement Action Using NLWs[6]

Scenario: In country C there has been a complete breakdown in law and order, and there is no functioning 'national' government. There is slaughter of communities, hunger and disease are rampant, abuse of fundamental human rights is commonplace, and local warlords and bandits are dominant and active with widespread fear and intimidation. There is a great clamour from the international community to 'do something' to stop the suffering of the civilian population. The Security Council authorizes a peace enforcement humanitarian intervention by the UNBIF military force. The task the UNBIF faces relates to the type of conflict. Its personnel may well be engaging opponents who are equipped with low-tech weaponry and who have few defences against sophisticated non-lethal weaponry, or their opponents may be armed with sophisticated countermeasures that can neutralize or minimize the effects of non-lethal weapons. For our purposes here, we will imagine that the warring factions do not have access to a sophisticated NLWs technology base. A UN Benign Intervention Force would be equipped with weaponry which did not contravene any international treaties and conventions, and its actions would be governed by international humanitarian law.

Objective: UNBIF Element 2: to intervene militarily to stop the fighting, separate the belligerents, enforce peace, and begin the movement and delivery of humanitarian relief. This is seen as a short-term mission, with as rapid transfer to Element 3 as possible. The thrust and primary emphasis of the enforcement element should be non-lethal.

Preconditions: An assumption is made that UNBIF permanent staff had adequate warning and time to map and analyse the conflict. The Security Council, in its mandate, had given clear political and military objectives and obtained the necessary support in the United Nations. Lines of command, communication[7] and accountability between UNBIF units and UN command in New York had been established, and all non-military avenues had been exhausted. UNBIF commanders have a wide range of non-lethal weapons at their disposal so that the combatants will not know what may be used against them next, and thus have less opportunity to create defences and countermeasures. The UNBIF is able rapidly to access pre-positioned stocks which include the most up-to-date protective equipment, both vehicular and personal protection armour.

For the purposes of this exercise the imaginary UNBIF campaign will be considered in seven phases. There would of course be overlap between these phases, 'a seamless progression' of events. The non-lethal weapons used in this scenario have been described in the earlier chapters.

Phase One: Intelligence gathering using satellites, unamanned aerial vehicles (UAV), spy planes, interception of communications (AWACS and JSTARS[8]), and on-the-spot intelligence. Of key importance to a successful campaign is not only the acquiring of intelligence, but also the ability to handle, analyse and quickly pass it on to field commanders. Strategic targets and positions are identified in advance so that prior strikes can be made to immobilize or deny them to the various factions before the UNBIF lands. Such targets would include ammunition dumps, high ground and airfields.

Phase Two: Before any attack is launched, the target military forces and the local civilian populations are given as much information as possible. Civilians can be provided with an accurate picture of the situation through TV and radio broadcasts. This can be done by interrupting domestic transmissions (see earlier), by electronic communication (for example via the Internet), and by dropping leaflets. Advances in technology mean that methods such as holographic projection and voice synthesis will soon be available. Using these methods, the form and sound of people who command the respect of those engaged in the conflict will be able to be artificially reproduced. Messages coming from such sources and images may be listened to and have more impact than those from an intervening force. Similarly, pleas can be made to warring factions for a ceasefire, and they can be warned against acts of inhumanity that could be interpreted as war crimes. The UNBIF propaganda will also aim to convince the factions that non-lethal weapons are effective.

Phase Three: Before the landing of the UNBIF, strategic targets are attacked with a wide range of non-lethal weapons delivered using UAVs, stealth and 'smart' technologies. The targets include: power grids which are neutralized by disrupting them with carbon fibres released from cruise missiles; weapons of mass destruction (WMD) such as biological and chemical agents, which are sprayed with agents that form tough, hard coats over them;[9] and radar and missile sites which are disrupted by electromagnetic pulses. Runways, roads and rail tracks needed for military logistics and supplies are made slippery and impassable by Teflon-type anti-traction agents; fuel dumps are contaminated by bacterial agents that degrade the petrol and diesel; and computer systems are invaded by computer viruses that attack software programmes, and also by ultra-fine carbon fibres that short-out and disrupt the computer hardware. Runways and roads are put out of action by dispersing four-spiked steel caltrops over them, which are cemented in place using hardening adhesives. Chemical embrittlement agents, which attack metallic components by weakening them and causing structural fracture, are applied to weapons and military installations. All these actions have the effect of denying military capability and degrading the military infrastructure.

Whilst the objective of these attacks is to frustrate and impede movement, the effects of non-lethal weapons on infrastructure and logistical routes must be reversible or it will be difficult for UNBIF troops to operate when they arrive on the scene.

Phase Four: Attacks on operational and tactical targets immediately prior to and during deployment of the UNBIF force. Landing sites must be secured and headquarters and command-and-control systems established. This is the most dangerous phase of the operation, when troops must make contact with the enemy. Non-lethal weapons that may find particular utility at this phase include optical munitions, psycho-chemicals, acoustic weapons, and incapacitating gases and chemicals. Superadhesives will be sprayed on tanks and other armoured vehicles to glue up their tracks, seal entry hatches and obscure viewing ports and optical sights. UAVs carrying microwave transmitters will disrupt and jam weapons, radar and communications systems, and enemy combatants will be sprayed with malodorous liquids, known as 'skunk shots', that inhibit military command and foment dissent (Scott, 1995). Special forces units will have been designated to rescue hostages. UNBIF base perimeter defences will include directional microwave transmitters that heat up to an unbearable temperature the skin of potential intruders who get too close, causing them to retreat; infrasound weapons which cause nausea and disorientation; and razor wire barriers covered in foam laced with chemical irritants and incapacitators.

During phases four and five the emphasis is on minimizing structural damage and loss of life.

Phase Five: Once the UNBIF has gained combat superiority, the job of separating the factions and enforcing the peace begins. This comprises a wide range of operations which may include: establishing ceasefire boundaries; enforcing a curfew; identifying and arresting war criminals; opening and protecting supply routes; confiscating heavy weapons and disarming combatants; controlling and defusing organized riots; and clearing mines.

UNBIF now moves from peace enforcement, and begins the handover to Benign Intervention Element 3, which has more a peace-keeping and policing function. However, whilst not on the streets, the UNBIF force is held in close reserve for a period of time.

Phase Six: Stabilizing the situation and beginning the clear-up of the effects of non-lethal weapons. Areas previously sprayed with anti-traction agents and other chemical non-lethal weapons must be cleared using solvents and antidotes. UN agencies and NGOs begin humanitarian aid delivery and the provision of health services, and priority is given to re-establishing independent media. To begin with, the press, radio and TV could be UN-organized, with the purpose of providing accurate information and news to the population, and also as part of 'winning the hearts and minds' of the people. Prisoner-of-war camps are built and guarded using UNBIF personnel, and a thorough investigation and accumulation of evidence of possible crimes against humanity is begun.

Phase Seven: Handover by UNBIF to Benign Intervention Element 3 units, whose role is more suited to peacekeeping and policing. UNBIF forces are held in reserve in case the situation deteriorates again. The long process of rebuilding the community and society begins.

Notes

1. *Inter Press Service International News*, 27 July 1995.
2. By July 1995, thirty-one countries had agreed to earmark troops for this purpose, and a further ten were seriously considering whether to do so.
3. Article 42 allows the UN 'to take such action by air, sea or land forces as may be necessary to maintain or restore international peace and security'.
4. The British Army *Wider Peacekeeping* manual (HMSO, 1995, pp. 2–8) defines consent as being supported by the principles of: impartiality, legitimacy, mutual respect, minimum force, credibility, and transparency.
5. See Goodwin-Gill and Cohn (1994).
6. Also see Barry, Everett and Peck (1994), p. 28.

7. See: Cooper, P, 'Bosnia C2 System To Bridge Allied Communications Gap', *Defense News*, 12–18 March 1996, for the degree of sophistication that can now be achieved in this area.

8. AWACS is short for Airborne Warning and Control Systems; JSTARS for Joint Surveillance Target Attack Radar Systems.

9. This is better than trying to destroy them with high explosives because of the danger these pose of spreading toxic or biologically active material.

6

Conclusion: The Future Role of Non-Lethal Weapons

Tomorrow's World, the BBC's popular science television series, ran a story on two US inventors of non-lethal weapons. From a box on the front bumper of their car, they launched what could best be described as a rocket-powered skateboard to which was attached electrical wires. The intention was to run the skateboard underneath the car in front – acting as a vehicle fleeing from the police at speed for the purposes of the test – and for the wires to short-out the car's electrical systems, so immobilizing it. In the first test the skateboard was ejected but veered off to the side of the road and missed the car by some distance. The second test could be considered a partial success as the skateboard easily caught up with the car. Unfortunately, there was a fault with the electrical wires that prevented a charge being successfully transferred, and both car and skateboard continued their journeys until the skateboard was caught up in the car's wheels.

The fact that millions of people will have seen the programme and been engaged, not to say amused, by these images tells us something about the state of popular perceptions around non-lethal weapons. Sticky guns and foam guns, aerosol sprays to cut out engines, mind-altering chemicals, and so on, bring with them reassuring images of use of force that is small-scale, discriminate, humane and with no lasting consequences for people or for the environment. How could anyone possibly object to weapons that provide an alternative to the guns, bombs, missiles, land mines and all the other facets of twentieth-century warfare that have brought with them so much death and destruction?

But our analysis leads us to challenge that narrow and simplistic interpretation of non-lethal weapons as benign, and view them in a much broader context. In the military arena, non-lethal weapons are primarily being developed to provide additional capabilities for conventional war fighting. A major military research effort has taken place with respect to lasers, acoustic weapons and other forms of directed energy weapons that can be used to incapacitate both personnel and equipment. Once the enemy is vulnerable and exposed, it can be defeated through lethal, conventional force.

Battlefield scenarios incorporating non-lethal weapons might see EMP cruise missiles launched against communication and sensor equipment as the first stage of an assault to degrade the enemy's ability to co-ordinate its forces. Laser weapons would be used to destroy optical equipment, coupled with isotropic/flash bombs exploded above enemy forces to dazzle and blind troops. Acoustic weapons would add to the troops' disorientation, inducing panic and attempts to flee defensive positions. As the combined effects of non-lethal weapons weakened the enemy, a range of conventional equipment including precision-guided munitions could be deployed to obtain a decisive outcome. So the dominant paradigm of non-lethal weapons, far from being small-scale and benign, brings with it images of full-scale warfare, of extreme pain and fear. Indeed, non-lethal warfare extends the range of potentially horrifying injuries, including blinding and damage to the internal organs, while in no way diminishing the traditional reliance on the use of lethal force. Environmental degradation, particularly through the effects of chemical and biological weapons, could be extensive and long-lasting.

This is not to deny that an intensive debate is developing about the nature of warfare in the twenty-first century (Cohen, 1996) and the role that non-lethal weapons might play in different scenarios to that of traditional war fighting. We explored one such scenario in Chapter 5. Many advocates of non-lethal weapons point to the growth of peacekeeping and peace enforcement operations where new military force structures are evidently needed but where, at present, effective alternative non-lethal weapons systems are not available. Equipping and training intervention forces with non-lethal weapons would, it is hoped, give commanders more options before having to resort to lethal force. In Somalia, for example, Operation Restore Hope quickly escalated from self-defence against snipers and rioters to offensive operations using helicopter gunships and special forces assault troops, and resulted in the deaths of many civilians. Somalia highlighted internal US political issues about the level of casualties, both to combatants and non-combatants, and also the role of the news media in potentially undermining support for military peace enforcement and peacekeeping operations. Referring to the advantage of non-lethal weapons in Operation United Shield, Colonel M. Stanton noted:

> We would like to see the development of nonlethal weapons as proof of our civility and restraint: nonlethal weapons show our reverence for life and our commitment to the use of minimal force. They show we are willing to go that extra mile to keep from having to kill anyone. The news coverage of these weapons prior to United Shield was almost universally positive. The military was bathed in the bright, approving glow of political correctness, because the new nonlethal technologies promised kinder, gentler operations other than war. (Stanton, 1996, p. 59)[1]

We can reasonably expect the role of peacekeeping and peace enforcement to be significant over the coming years but, as we have stressed, care must be taken to discriminate between the two. Recent events illustrate the range of potential operations. In Bosnia, the UN peacekeeping force faced well-trained and well-armed forces who simply ignored internationally negotiated ceasefires and safe havens and other peace initiatives, and who openly abused international humanitarian law and other accepted norms of civilized behaviour. It is not surprising that UN military commanders experienced growing frustration at their ineffectiveness and pushed for the use of conventional attacks such as aerial bombing and heavy artillery strikes, nor that the Peace Implementation Force (IFOR) deployed to oversee the Dayton peace agreement had conventional military rules of engagement. By contrast, other peace support operations are relatively small-scale – such as the monitoring of the transition to democracy in Haiti and the peacekeeping operation in Cyprus – and involve little direct military confrontation.

During peace enforcement actions, it is doubtful that military commanders would ever give up the option of conventional lethal force; therefore the deployment of non-lethal weapons would simply be another option to consider dependent on the military situation. For peacekeeping, however, non-lethal weapons represent a capability that is qualitatively different from the use of conventional force. The general framework for peacekeeping is based around consent, and in this policing role non-lethal weapons should be deployed as weapons of first choice before any resort to lethal force is considered. The ethos of peacekeeping by consent must be to minimize the number of casualties and the seriousness of their injuries. In Chapter 5 we glanced at the debate surrounding the possible demilitarization of peacekeeping operations. Peacekeeping in the future will remain a complex and messy affair that raises many issues about how a UN Benign Intervention Force might operate. Common problems in such operations include the use of civilians by all sides to thwart, for example, the delivery of humanitarian aid to opposing factions by blocking roads or intermingling fighters and civilians. Non-lethal weapons will find greater utility with commanders in separating combatants and non-combatants, and for clearing with minimum injury such human roadblocks. So, if non-lethal weapons can play a role in diffusing potentially dangerous situations, while enhancing the legitimacy of peacekeeping operations, then they deserve consideration.

Two serious issues are raised by the use of non-lethal weapons. First, the blurring of distinctions between military and civil security operations and, second, the impact on existing international treaties and weapons conventions. Significantly, a major non-lethal weapons programme in the USA that is run jointly by the Department of Defense and the Department of Justice is expected to provide new weapons for both the military and the police. An obvious danger is that civil security becomes increasingly militarized as the police deploy a sophisticated array of weapons and use military-style tactics and operational behaviour. The traditional relationship of the police to the public as a civil force would come under further pressure. An added complication is the role that civil operations may play in circumventing international treaties and conventions prohibiting the use in war of certain types of weapons, most obviously chemical and biological weapons. If new riot control agents are deployed for civil security, it would prove extremely difficult in practice to prevent their military use. One great danger with non-lethal weapons is that, quite simply, they ride a coach and horses through both the spirit and the letter of major weapons conventions. These include the UN Inhumane Weapons Convention and the Biological and Chemical Weapons Conventions, which represent the best hope the international community has for the abolition of certain types of weapons that are considered to inflict indiscriminate, unnecessary and superfluous injury and, in some cases, are classified as potential weapons of mass destruction.

Some advocates of non-lethal weapons recognize these dilemmas (many simply ignore them), but argue that the existing conventions should not apply to non-lethal weapons. Most of these weapons were considered science fiction, or not even dreamed of, when the treaties were initially designed. Clearly, Cold War chemical and biological warfare capabilities, and those identified in the Iraqi arsenal during the Gulf War, were intended as weapons of mass destruction. Non-lethal chemical and biological weapons are intended to be temporarily disabling and to have no long-lasting effects (at least in theory). But these operational differences should not disguise how similar many of the compounds and agents used for traditional weapons are to those in NLWs. Development and deployment of chemical and biological warfare agents could take place under the guise of NLWs and it would be impossible, in practice, to differentiate between non-lethal and lethal weapons. The case of riot control agents has already been mentioned. Years of painstaking work on these conventions would be put in jeopardy.

Similar concerns exist about other major non-lethal weapons including lasers and acoustic weapons. In Chapter 4 we looked at blinding lasers, which have been the subject of an international campaign led by organizations such as the International Red Cross and the Human Rights Watch Arms Project to have them banned. But a complicating factor is that the military utility of lasers is now well established both for range-finding and as anti-optical equipment weapons. Some mechanism has to be found that distinguishes conventional lasers from blinding lasers, since military commanders are unlikely to give up such capabilities without effective substitutes. Little attention has been given to acoustic weapons, since there have been no major deployments, but their effects are potentially as serious and long-lasting on the internal organs of the body, and could be as horrifying. They illustrate how difficult it is for the international community's efforts at conventions and arms control to accommodate weapons innovation. In some cases it is not enough to tinker with existing arms control agreements; it will become necessary to write completely new ones.

For all the attempts to market non-lethal weapons as new and different, what they really represent is the latest in a long line of weapons development based on the belief that advanced technology is the basis for military superiority. Although non-lethal weapons R&D may be relatively small-scale in comparison to other forms of conventional research, it is playing a growing role in sustaining both high levels of military R&D overall and high levels of military spending. An added factor is the level of secrecy surrounding some forms of non-lethal weapons research. For obvious reasons, such as the fear of countermeasures, military planners would prefer to limit the publicly available information on the capabilities of new weapons under research. The steady growth of 'black' programmes in the USA includes some non-lethal weapons, but we can only speculate on their potential application.

We have similar concerns regarding the radical school of non-lethal weapons advocates, who project NLWs not just as an additional capability to conventional warfare, but as a revolutionary catalyst that will alter the very nature of war fighting towards a more benign arena in the twenty-first century. At one level, we could simply dismiss such thinking as speculative since the dominant paradigm of non-lethal weapons places them at a supplementary and subordinate level to conventional weapons. But such visions do have a real significance that transcend the prospects, or more accurately the lack of prospects, for radical changes to take place. The very fact that military specialists and analysts can argue for fundamental changes in the structure and operations of the armed forces, while acknowledging that there is little likelihood of their implementation, deserves some comment. Not only does it represent deep-lying concerns that the world has entered a dangerous phase of both international and intra-national conflict, characterized as the 'age of chaos', it also seems to encapsulate a sense that the West will be impotent to resolve these sorts of conflicts in its favour through traditional military means. For military planners that is unacceptable, hence the attraction of a new generation of weapons that seem to offer the potential for a new form of warfare. This might be described as 'societal war', a reconceptualization of total war, in which the major civil assets of an adversary are targeted as well as its military forces and structures. For some advocates of non-lethal weapons, that offers the West the potential for strategic paralysis of an enemy's civilian infrastructure and economy.

Here, non-lethal weapons can be viewed as a 'technological fix' to twenty-first-century conflict, just as Star Wars in the 1980s reflected a similar response to frustrations over the threat of ballistic missile attack despite the obvious fact that a comprehensive anti-ballistic missile defence system was unattainable. Fundamentally, non-lethal weapons do nothing to change the dominant military paradigm of security, which looks to maintain superiority over potential adversaries through military technological advantage. Even the more radical visions of twenty-first-century warfare without the use of conventional force, nevertheless celebrate the application of military technology; according to this vision battles are to be fought with non-lethal weapons systems by remote control.

For there to be any real hope of the international community, through the UN, addressing these issues, the UN itself must undergo radical reform. This must include a restructuring of the Security Council to more accurately reflect the composition and needs of the UN General Assembly. Part of this restructuring could be the formation of a force such as the UN Benign Intervention Force we conceptualized in Chapter 5, backed by the necessary military and political command structures at UN headquarters. Related to this must be the formulation of clear ethical criteria and guidelines for the use of such intervention forces, and these must be worked out in partnership with the NGO community and UN agencies. But we must not accept the dominant ethos of the military in conflict resolution, and we must continue efforts to move away from reliance on military solutions. There is a case to be made for demilitarizing the UN completely. Information on any weapons to be used by a force such as a UN Benign Intervention Force must be in the public domain, and weapons R&D must be assessed by strict criteria regarding their action and effects, and within the framework of existing weapons conventions. A UN force would also need its own, and distinct, rules of engagement through sophisticated channels of accountability and control. Ultimately, any peacekeeping operations should be in the context of a major UN preventative economic development model and within the framework and ethos of Benign Intervention.

Whilst much of this book has focused on military applications of non-lethal weapons, we also noted their growing significance in civil police use. In this area there can be no doubt that they have utility, for example in the protection of law enforcement officers and in the restraint and arrest of violent criminals. Society asks police agencies to perform an increasingly difficult task which we expect them to perform as humanely as possible, and to do this they should have access to appropriate non-lethal weapons. In Chapter 4 we examined some of the potential dangers connected with this. Several issues are relevant here. Some would argue that non-lethal weapons technology can provide an authoritarian state with more means of oppressing and controlling people, and give police more tools for the abuse of power. Other opponents, referring to 'preventive' surveillance and information-gathering techniques that are developing from non-lethal technology, claim that these are yet further infringements of personal privacy and human rights.

We have seen that the rapid advances in technology that are making available a new generation of non-lethal weapons raises issues that span a broad spectrum of concerns. There is a real dilemma here. On the one hand there are those who earnestly see non-lethal weapons as a means of making war fighting more humane and less destructive, whilst on the other there is the powerful military-industrial research complex determined to exploit this technology to bolster its own power and influence, and to help maintain a strong weapons research infrastructure. For some in the latter group, non-lethal weapons are seen as making killing easier and quicker. It is important that accountability for non-lethal weapons programmes is ensured. Non-lethal weapons R&D is proceeding quickly and it is essential that their development is watched because there are serious implications for undermining existing weapons conventions, and sinister aspects which relate to the social control of populations. Some non-lethal weapons, such as electric shock batons, are sold to customers who are known to use them for the purposes of torture.[2]

We have to resist the fatal attraction that NLWs transcend concerns surrounding conventional weapons, and the dilemmas surrounding the use of force. They are simply weapons, and it would be dangerous not to treat them in the same way as any other weapon.

Notes

1. Colonel Stanton had previous experience in Somalia, where he served as an infantry battalion operations officer with Operation Restore Hope.
2. Channel 4 (UK) *Dispatches* programmes on 6 March and 13 March 1996.

Appendix

Non-Lethal Weapons:
Recent Policy and Operational Influences

1940s–1950s	245T herbicides used by British army in Malaya
1961	CS gas used by British army in Cyprus
1965	Chemical Mace used by US law enforcement agencies
May 1970	Report by Joseph Coates for the US Institute for Defense Analyses, Science and Technology Division: 'Nonlethal and Nondestructive Combat in Cities Overseas'
June 1970	Rubber bullets first used in Northern Ireland
March 1972	Report prepared by Security Planning Corporation for the US National Science Foundation: 'Nonlethal Weapons for Law Enforcement: Research Needs and Priorities'
June 1986	US Attorney-General organizes conference on: 'Less-Than-Lethal Weapons'
1991	Cruise missiles armed with carbon fibres used in the Gulf War
March 1991	US Defense Secretary Cheney establishes a Non-Lethal Warfare Study Group
1994	Paper by Janet and Chris Morris: 'Nonlethality: A Global Strategy'

January 1994	NATO Non-Lethal Study Group set up
April 1994	Revolution in Military Affairs Group set up, chaired by US Deputy Defense Secretary John Deutsch
January 1995	US Marines equipped with non-lethal weapons in Somalia
May 1995	US Commission on Roles and Missions identified a role for non-lethal weapons in high-priority missions
June 1995	US DoD draft policy directive on roles, acquisition, and operational utility of non-lethal weapons
June 1995	US Council for Foreign Relations report: 'Non-Lethal Technologies: Military Options and Implications'
July 1995	National Technology Transfer Center (NASA) and National Institute for Justice (US Justice Department) set up joint project to review non-lethal weapons technologies. Project is managed by NIJ's Office of Law Enforcement and Technology Commercialization

Bibliography

Ackroyd, C. et al. (1977) *The Technology of Political Control*, Penguin Books, London.

Aftergood, S. (1994) 'The Soft-Kill Fallacy', *Bulletin of the Atomic Scientists*, Vol. 50, No. 5, pp. 40–45.

Aftergood, S. (1995) 'Monitoring Emerging Military Technologies' and 'A Revolution in Military Affairs', *FAS Public Interest Report*, Vol. 48, No. 1, January/February, pp. 1–14.

Alexander, J. (1993) *Nonlethal Weapons and Limited Force Options*, Paper presented to US Council on Foreign Relations, New York, NY, October.

Alexander, J. (1995) *Non-lethal Weapons and the Future of War*, Paper presented to Harvard MIT Seminar on the Future of War, John M. Olin Institute for Strategic Studies, Harvard, March.

Alexander, J. (n.d.) *Rethinking National Security Requirements and The Need For Non-lethal Weapons Options*, Submitted to President-Elect Clinton's Transition Team. Los Alamos National Laboratory.

Anderberg, B. and Wolbarsht, M. (1990) 'Blinding Lasers: The Next Weapon?', *Military Technology*, March.

Applegate, R. (1969) *Riot Control – Materiel and Techniques*, Stackpole Books, Harrisburg.

Applegate, R. (1971) 'Nonlethal Police Weapons', *Ordnance*, July–August, pp. 62–6.

Arkin, B. (1995) 'Ban Tactical Laser Weapons', *Defense News*, 17/23 July.

ARPA (Advanced Research Projects Agency) (1993), *Program Information Package for Defense Technology Conversion, Reinvestment, and Transition Assistance*, Washington DC.

Aviation Week and Space Technology (1992) 'Nonlethal Weapons Give Peacekeepers Flexibility', 7 December, pp. 50–51.

Ballantyne, R. (1996) 'It'll All End in Tears', *Guardian*, 11 January, pp. 8–9.

Barry, J. and Morgenthau, T. (1994) 'Soon "Phasers on Stun"', *Newsweek*, 7 February, pp. 30–31.

Barry, J., Everett, M. and Peck, A. (1994) *Nonlethal Military Means: New Leverage for a New Era*, National Security Program Policy Analysis Paper 94–101, John F. Kennedy School of Government, Harvard University.

Bartlett, H., Holman, G. and Somes, E. (1995) 'The Art of Strategy and Force Planning', *Naval War College Review*, Vol. XLVIII, No. 2, Spring, pp. 114–26.

Barzilay, D. (1973) *The British Army in Ulster, Vol. 1*, Century Books, Belfast.

Beard, E. (1976) *Developing the ICBM – A Study in Bureaucratic Politics*, Columbia University Press, New York.

Beaumont, P. (1994) 'Non-lethal Weapon', *Observer*, *Life* section, 9 October, p. 2.

Becker, J. and Heal, C. (1996) 'Less-Than-Lethal Force: Doctrine Must Lead the Technology Rush', *Jane's International Defense Review*, February, pp. 62–4.

Bennis, P. (1994) 'Blue Helmets. For What? Under Whom?'. In Childers, E. (ed.) *Challenges to the United Nations: Building A Safer World*, CIIR/St Martin's Press, London, pp. 152–75.

Berkowitz, B. (1994) 'Rules of Engagement for UN Peacekeeping Forces in Bosnia', *Orbis*, Fall, pp. 635–46.

Best, G. (1983) *Humanity in Warfare: The Modern History of International Law in Armed Conflict*, Methuen, London.

Blix, H. (1974) 'Current Efforts to Prohibit the Use of Certain Conventional Weapons', *Instant Research on Peace and Violence*, Vol. 4, No. 1, pp. 21–30.

Blunden, M., Greene, O. and Naughton, J. (1989) 'The Alchemists of Our Time: The Weapons Scientist as Scapegoat', in Blunden, M. and Greene, O. (eds) *Science and Mythology in the Making of Defence Policy*, Brassey's, London.

BMD Monitor (1985) 'Advanced Weapons is a Growth Area at Phillips', 16 June.

Boseley, S. (1993) 'Ethics, sans Frontieres', *Guardian*, 2 September.

Boutros-Ghali, Boutros (1992) *An Agenda for Peace: Preventive Diplomacy, Peace-making and Peace-Keeping*, United Nations, New York.

Boutwell, J., Klare, M. and Reed, L. (1995) *Lethal Commerce: The Global Trade in Small Arms and Light Weapons*, American Academy of Arts and Sciences, Cambridge, MA.

British Army Doctrine Publication. Volume 1: Operations (1994) HQDT/18/34/46. Army Code No. 71565 Pt 1, Ministry of Defence, June.

Builder, C.H. (1995) 'Looking in All the Wrong Places? The Real Revolution in Military Affairs is Staring Us in the Face', *Armed Forces Journal International*, May, pp. 38–9.

Bunker, R and Moore, T.L. (1996) *Nonlethal Technology and Fourth Epoch War: A New Paradigm of Politico-Military Force*, Land Warfare Paper No. 23, Institute of Land Warfare, Association of the United States Army, Arlington, VA.

Burk, J. (ed.) (1994) *The Military in New Times: Adapting Armed Forces to a Turbulent World*, Westview Press, Boulder, CO.

Campbell, D. (1996). 'Police Test CS Sprays to Combat Violence', *Guardian*, 19 February.

Capaccio, T. (1995a) 'US Commanders State Uses For Non-Lethal Technology', *Defense Week*, 23 January, pp. 3, 14.

Capaccio, T. (1995b) 'Non-Lethal Acquisition Plan in the Works', *Defense Week*, 21 August, pp. 1, 9.

Childers, E. (ed.) (1994) *Challenges to the United Nations: Building A Safer World*, CIIR/St Martin's Press, London.

Clarke, J. (1995) 'The Enforcement Specialists', *Armed Forces Journal International*, February, pp. 34–5.

Cleveland, H (ed.) (1993) *New Strategies for a Restless World*, American Refugee Committee, Minneapolis, MN. Chapter 5: 'The Law of Humanitarian Intervention', by Nancy Arnison, and Chapter 6: 'The Military Role in Emergency Response', by Arthur Dewey.

Coates, J.F. (1970) *Nonlethal and Nondestructive Combat in Cities Overseas*, Institute for Defence Analysis, Science and Technology Division, Arlington, VA, May.

Coates, J.F. (1972) 'Non-Lethal Police Weapons', *Technology Review*, June, pp. 49–56.

Cobey, J., Flanagin, A. and Foege, W. (1993) 'Effective Humanitarian Aid. Our Only Hope for Intervention in Civil War', *Journal of American Medical Association*, 4 August, pp. 632–4.

Cohen, E. (1994) 'The Mystique of US Air Power', *Foreign Affairs*, January/ February, pp. 109–24.

Cohen, E. (1996) 'A Revolution in Warfare', *Foreign Affairs*, March/April, Vol. 75, No. 2, pp. 37–54.

Collins, J.M. (1995) *Nonlethal Weapons and Operations: Potential Applications and Practical Limitations*, Library of Congress, Washington: Congressional Research Service Report for Congress, 14 September.

Conetta, C. and Knight, C. (1995) *Vital Force: A Proposal for the Overhaul of the UN Peace Operations System and for the Creation of a UN Legion*, Massachusetts: Project on Defense Initiatives, Commonwealth Institute.

Cook, J.W., Fiely, D. and McGowan, M. (1995) 'NonLethal Weapons: Technologies, Legalities, and Potential Policies', *Airpower Journal*, Special Issue, pp. 77–91.

Cooper, P. (1995a) 'US Enhances Mind Games', *Defense News*, 17–23 April, p. 12.

Cooper, P. (1995b) 'Nonlethals Get Funding Plan', *Defense News*, 24–30 July.

Cornish, P. (1995) 'Inhumane Weapons: 1995 Review of the UN Weaponry Convention', *Bulletin of Arms Control*, No. 18, June, pp. 3–7.

Council for Foreign Relations. (1995) *Non-lethal Technologies: Military Options and Implications*, Report of an Independent Task Force, Council for Foreign Relations, Washington DC.

Coupland, R. (1996) 'The Effect of Weapons: Defining Superfluous Injury and Unnecessary Suffering', *Medicine and Global Survival*, March. Internet: http://www.healthnet.org/MGS/MGS.html.

Cox, E. (1995) *Non-lethal Weapons*, Peace Action Education Fund Briefing Paper, USA, July.

Curtis, L. (1987) *They Shoot Children: The Use of Rubber and Plastic Bullets in the North of Ireland*, 2nd edn, Information on Ireland, London.

Deane-Drummond, A. (1975) *Riot Control*, Royal United Services Institute for Defence Studies, London.

Dedring, J. (1994) *Humanitarian Interventions by the United Nations*, Department of Humanitarian Affairs, United Nations, New York.

Deen, T. (1995) 'Disarmament: Shoot But Don't Kill, Experts Tell US Forces', *Armed Forces Newswire Service*, 17 July.

Defense Daily, (1995) 'ARPA Wants Proposals for Developing Non-lethal Technologies', 2 May.

Department of Defense (US) (1994) *Department of Defense in-House R&D Activities – Management Analysis Report for Fiscal Year 1993*, Washington DC.

Dewar, M. (1985) *The British Army in Northern Ireland*, Arms and Armour Press, London.

Dewar, M. (1995) *Weapons and Equipment of Counter-Terrorism*, Arms and Armour Press, London.

Donald, D. and Hayes, B. (eds) (1995) *Beyond Traditional Peacekeeping*, Macmillan, London. Chapter 1: 'On The Brink of a New Era? Humanitarian Interventions', by Thomas Weiss; Chapter 8: 'Structural Issues and the Future of UN Peace Operations' by William Durch; Chapter 9: 'UN Peace Support Operations: Political–Military Considerations', by Jim Whitman and Ian Bartholomew; Chapter 10: 'Military Issues in Multinational Operations', by Margaret Cecchine Harrell and Robert Howe.

Doswald-Beck, L. (ed.) (1993) *Blinding Weapons: Reports of the Meetings of Experts Convened by the International Committee of the Red Cross on Battlefield Laser Weapons, 1989–1991*, ICRC, Geneva.

Doswald-Beck, L. and Vite, S. (1993). 'International Humanitarian Law and Human Rights Law', *International Review of the Red Cross*, No. 293, March–April, pp. 94–119.

Eberle, J. (1993) 'Military Aspects of "An Agenda for Peace"', in *Memorandum on 'An Agenda for Peace': The Expanding Role of the United Nations and the Implications for UK Policy*, United Nations Association (UK), London, Appendix 1.

Economist (1995), 'Defence Technology: Information Warfare Survey', June, pp. 18–20.

Egner, D.O. et al. (1977) *The Evolution of Less-lethal Weapons*, Human Engineering Laboratory, Aberdeen Proving Grounds, Maryland, December.

Eide, A. (1976) 'Outlawing the Use of Some Conventional Weapons – Another Approach to Disarmament?', *Instant Research on Peace and Violence*, Vol. 6, No. 1–2, pp. 39–51.

Elliot, V. (1995) 'Condon Calls for Police Pepper Sprays', *Sunday Telegraph*, 18 June.

Evancoe, P. (1993) 'Non-lethal Technologies Enhance Warrior's Punch', *National Defense*, December, pp. 27–9.

Faul, D. and Murray, R. (1981) *Rubber and Plastic Bullets Kill and Maim*, Association for Legal Justice, Belfast.

Federal News Service, (1995) *Defense Department Background Briefing Regarding Non-Lethal Weapons. Attributable to a Senior Military Official, The Pentagon*, Washington DC, 17 February.

Federal Union. (1960) *Proposals for a Permanent United Nations Force*, Federal Union, London.

Fenrick, W.J. (1990) 'The Conventional Weapons Convention: A Modest But Useful Treaty', *International Review of the Red Cross*, No. 279, November–December, pp. 498–509.

Fessler, A. (1995) 'Benign Intervention – An Idea Whose Time Has Come?', *Friends' Quarterly*, Vol. 29, No. 6, April, pp. 246–55.

Fields, R. (1977) *Society Under Siege: A Psychology of Northern Ireland*, Temple University Press, Philadelphia.

Fishetti, M. (1995) 'Less-Than-Lethal Weapons', *Technology Review*, 14 January.

Fox, B. (1995) 'Kind Control', *New Scientist*, 25 November, p. 26.

Frost, G. and Shipbaugh, C. (1994), *GPS Targeting Methods for Non-lethal Systems*, Rand Publication RP-262, Santa Monica, CA.

Fukuyama, F. (1992) *The End of History and the Last Man*, Penguin, London.

Fulghum, D.A. (1993a) 'ALCMs Given Non-lethal Role', *Aviation Week and Space Technology*, 22 February, p. 20.

Fulghum, D.A. (1993b) 'EMP Weapons Lead Non-lethal Technology', *Aviation Week and Space Technology*, 24 May, p. 61.

Girard, H. (1995a) 'Human Experiments', Letter in *SGR Newsletter*, Issue 9, June.

Girard, H. (1995a) *Non-lethal Weapons Policy: The Case of Electromagnetic Weapons*, Paper presented at the Annual Meeting of the Canadian Association for Security and Intelligence Studies, University of Quebec, 5 June.

Goldblat, J. (1970) 'Are Tear Gas and Herbicides Permitted Weapons?', *Bulletin of the Atomic Scientists*, April, pp. 13–16.

Goldblat, J. (1978) *Arms Control: A Survey and Appraisal of Multilateral Agreements*, SIPRI/Taylor & Francis Ltd, London.

Goldblat, J. (1995) 'Inhumane Conventional Weapons. Efforts to Strengthen Constraints', *Arms, Disarmament and International Security*, SIPRI, Stockholm, pp. 825–35.

Goodwin-Gill, G. and Cohn, I. (1994) *Child Soldiers: The Role of Children in Armed Conflict*, Clarendon Press, Oxford.

Gordenker, L. and Weiss, T. (eds) (1991) *Soldiers, Peacekeepers and Disasters*, International Peace Academy/Macmillan, New York.

Gordon, P. (1987) 'The Killing Machine: Britain and the International Repression Trade', *Race and Class*, Vol. XXIX, No. 2, pp. 31–52.

Graham, M. (1987) *Cruise Missile Development in the USA Since the Early 1970s – A Case Study of the Determinants of Weapons Succession*, unpublished PhD thesis, Science Policy Research Unit, Sussex University, Brighton.

Green, L.C. (1993) *The Contemporary Law of Armed Conflict*, Manchester University Press, Manchester.

Hall, W.M. (1985) 'A Critique of the Doctrine-Training Fit', *Military Review*, June, pp. 30–57.

Harris, R. and Paxman, J. (1982) *A Higher Form of Killing: The Secret Story of Gas and Germ Warfare*, Chatto & Windus, London.

Haseley, D. (1992) 'TRADOC Drafting Concept for Infusing Non-lethal Warfare into Army Doctrine', *Inside the Army*, 24 February, p. 7.

Hay, A. (1996). 'Coming Clean on CS Gas', *Guardian*, 1 February.

Hecker, S. (1994) 'Retargeting the Weapons Laboratories', *Issues in Science and*

Technology, Vol. 10, No. 4, pp. 44–51.

Hewish, M. (1994) 'Put the Use into Dual Use', *International Defence Review*, Vol. 27, No. 1, January.

Hewish, M (1995) 'Battlefield Lasers – The Race Between Action and Countermeasure', *International Defence Review*, Vol. 28, No. 2. pp. 39–40.

Hewish, M. and Pengelley, R. (1994) 'New Age Soldiering', *International Defense Review*, Vol. 27, No. 1, January, pp. 26–33.

Hitchins, T. (1994) 'DoD Nonlethal Effort Fuels Fear of Treaty Violations', *Defence News*, 26 September–2 October.

HMSO (1995) *Wider Peacekeeping (The Army Field Manual Volume 5: Operations Other Than War, Part 2)*, HMSO, London.

Hoffmann, W. (ed.) (1991) *A New World Order. Can It Bring Security to the World's People?: Essays on Restructuring the United Nations*, World Federalist Association, Washington DC. Chapter 2: 'Should There Be a Standing UN Police Force? Or a UN Peacekeeping Reserve?', by Kathryn Damm.

Hoshen, J., Sennott, J. and Winkler, M. (1995) 'Keeping Tabs On Criminals', *IEEE Spectrum*, February, pp. 26–32.

Human Rights Watch Arms Project (1995a) *US Blinding Laser Weapons*, Human Rights Watch, Washington DC, Vol. 7, No. 5, May.

Human Rights Watch Arms Project (1995b) *Blinding Laser Weapons: The Need to Ban a Cruel and Inhumane Weapon*, Human Rights Watch, September.

Huntington, S. (1993) 'The Clash of Civilizations', *Foreign Affairs*, Summer, Vol. 72, No. 3, pp. 22–49.

ICEUSCI (International Commission of Enquiry into US Crimes in Indochina) (1972) *The Effects of Modern Weapons on the Human Environment in Indochina*, International Commission of Enquiry into US Crimes in Indochina, Stockholm.

ICRC (International Committee of the Red Cross) (1949) *The Geneva Conventions of August 12 1949*, ICRC, Geneva.

ICRC (International Committee of the Red Cross) (1977) *Protocols Additional to the Geneva Conventions of 12 August 1949*, ICRC, Geneva.

ICRC (International Committee of the Red Cross) (1993), *Blinding Weapons: Reports of the Meeting of Experts Convened by the International Committee of the Red Cross on Battlefield Laser Weapons 1989–1991*, ICRC, Geneva.

ICRC (International Committee of the Red Cross) (1994), *Expert Meeting on Certain Weapon Systems and on Implementation Mechanisms in International Law. Report of Meeting, Geneva 30 May–1 June 1994*, ICRC, Geneva, July. Especially the following: Liszka, L., 'Sonic Beam Devices – Principles', pp. 89–91; Perry Robinson, J., 'Developments in "Non-Lethal Weapons" Involving Chemicals', pp. 92–7; Bartfai, T. et al., 'Benefits and Threats of Developments in Biotechnology and Genetic Engineering', pp. 98–112; Tuor, S. and Morton, S., 'Future Weapons Using High Power Microwaves', pp. 113–19; Dutli, M.T., 'Mechanisms for the Implementation of International Humanitarian Law', pp. 120–27; Hampson, F., 'Monitoring and Enforcement Mechanisms in the Human Rights Field', pp. 128–33.

ICRC (International Committee of the Red Cross) (1995) *Blinding Lasers: Questions and Answers*, Briefing Document, ICRC, Geneva.

Inside the Army (1995) 'Army Develops Doctrinal Framework for Use of Non-lethal Capabilities', and 'Draft Concept for Non-lethal Capabilities in Army Operations', 31 July, pp. 1, 13–19.

Inside the Navy (1995) 'Draft Policy for Non-lethal Weapons', 17 July, pp. 8–9.

Inside the Pentagon (1995), Vol. 11, No. 28, 13 July.

Jane's Defence Weekly (1994) 'US Group to Assess Military Revolution', 16 April.

Jannery, B. (1995) 'No "Silver Bullet" Solution In Less-lethal Weapons, Marine Corps Says', 17 July, pp. 7–8.

Jean, F (ed.) (1993) *Life, Death and Aid: The Médecins Sans Frontières Report on World Crisis Interventions*, Routledge, London.

Kalshoven, F. (1987) *Constraints on the Waging of War*, ICRC, Geneva.

Kalshoven, F. (1990) 'The Conventional Weapons Convention: Underlying Legal Principles', *International Review of the Red Cross*, No. 279, November–December, pp. 510–20.

Kanter, A. and Brooks, L. (eds) (1994) *US Intervention Policy for the Post-Cold War World: New Challenges and Responses*, W.W. Norton, New York. Chapter 3: 'Adapting Conventional Military Forces to the New Environment', by John O.B. Sewall; Chapter 4: 'New Applications of Nonlethal and Less Lethal Technology', by Richard Garwin.

Kennedy, P. (1988) *The Rise and Fall of the Great Powers: Economic Change and Military Conflict from 1500–2000*, Unwin Hyman, London.

Kenney, G. and Dugan, M. (1992) 'Operation Balkans Storm: Here's a Plan', *New York Times*, 29 November.

Kiernan, V. (1994) 'ARPA Seeks Cheaper, Better Laser Weapons', *Laser Focus World*, July, p. 53.

Kitson, F. (1971) *Low Intensity Operations: Subversion, Insurgency, Peace-keeping*, Faber & Faber, London.

Klaaren, J. and Mitchell, R. (1995) 'Nonlethal Technology and Airpower: A Winning Combination for Strategic Paralysis', *Airpower Journal*, Special Edition, pp. 42–51.

Knoth, A. (1994) 'Disabling Technologies: A Critical Assessment', *International Defense Review*, July, pp. 30–39.

Kokoski, R. (1994) 'Non-lethal Weapons: A Case Study of New Technology Developments', *SIPRI Yearbook 1994: World Armaments and Disarmament*, Oxford University Press, Oxford, pp. 367–86.

Krepon, M. (1974) 'Weapons Potentially Inhumane: The Case Of Cluster Bombs', *Foreign Affairs*, Vol. 52, No. 3, April, pp. 595–611.

Lamb, C. (1994) 'Non-lethal Weapons Policy: Department of Defense Directive', 1 January.

Lancet (1994) Editorial: 'Weapons Intended to Blind', 17 December.

Lawrence Livermore National Laboratory (1994), 'The State of the Laboratory', *Energy and Technology Review*, January/February 1994.

Lessard, P. (1995) 'Groups Unveil Plan to Deploy Technology in Fighting Crime', *Federal Technology Report*, 20 July.

Levie, H.S. (1986) *The Code of International Armed Conflict*, Oceana, New York.

Lewer, N. (1995) 'Non-Lethal Weapons', *Medicine and War*, Vol. 11, No. 2, pp. 78–90.

Lewer, N. and Ramsbotham, O. (1993) *'Something Must be Done': Towards an Ethical Framework for Humanitarian Intervention in International Social Conflict,* Peace Research Report Number 33, Department of Peace Studies, University of Bradford, August, pp. 125.

Lorenz, F.M. (1995) 'Less-lethal Force in Operation United Shield', *Marine Corps Gazette,* September, pp. 69–76.

Louise, C. (1995) *The Social Impacts of Light Weapons Availability and Proliferation,* UNRISD Discussion Paper No. 59, March.

Luce, E. (1994) 'TV Sets Aid Agenda says Red Cross', *Guardian,* 14 October.

Luce, E. and Fairhall, D. (1994) 'Call to Ban New Guns that Blind', *Guardian,* February 19.

Lumsden, M. (1974) ' New Military Technology and the Erosion of International Law: The Case of the Dum-Dum Bullets Today', *Instant Research on Peace and Violence,* Vol. 4, No. 1, pp. 15–20.

Lumsden, M. (1978) *Anti-personnel Weapons,* SIPRI/Taylor & Francis, London.

Mackinlay, J. (1994) 'Improving Multinational Forces', *Survival,* Autumn.

MacPherson, K. (1994) '500,000 Endangered by Tests since 1940', *Washington Times,* 29 September, p. A9.

Magyar, K.P. (ed.) (1994) *Challenge and Response: Anticipating US Military Security Concerns,* Air University Press, Alabama, August. See especially O'Connor, P.G., 'Waging War With Nonlethal Weapons', pp. 333–46.

Markusen, A. and Yudken, J. (1992) *Dismantling the Cold War Economy,* Basic Books, New York.

Maurice, A. (1990) 'The International Committee and the Problem of Excessively Injurious or Indiscriminate Weapons', *International Review of the Red Cross,* No. 279, November–December, pp. 477–97.

Mazarr, M.J. (1993) *The Military Technical Revolution: A Structural Framework,* Final Report of the CSIS Study Group on the MTR. Center for Strategic and International Studies, Washington DC, March.

Metz, S. and Kievit, J. (1994) *The Revolution in Military Affairs and Conflict Short of War,* Strategic Studies Institute, US Army War College, 25 July.

Metz, S. and Kievet, J. (1995) *Strategy and Revolution in Military Affairs. From Theory to Policy,* draft version, Strategic Studies Institute, US Army War College, 27 June.

Meyer, M. (1987) 'Humanitarian Action: A Delicate Balancing Act', *International Review of the Red Cross,* September–October, No. 260, pp. 485–500.

Miliband, R. and Panitch, L. (1994) *Socialist Register 1994 – Between Globalism and Nationalism,* Merlin Press, London.

Millar, R. et al. (1975) 'Injuries Caused by Rubber Bullets: A Report on 90 Patients', *British Journal of Surgery,* Vol. 62, pp. 480–86.

Miller, A. (1992) 'No Safe Haven? Kurdish Relief Operation April–July 1991', *Journal of Royal Naval Medical Service,* Vol. 78, No. 2, pp. 81–6.

Miller, A. and Kershaw, C. (1993) 'Initial Medical Reception, Intervention and Survey Work in Combined Military and Civilian Humanitarian Aid: Operation "Safe Haven", Northern Iraq', *Medicine and War,* Vol. 9, No. 1, pp. 24–32.

Minnear, L. and Weiss, T. (1995) *Mercy Under Fire: War and the Global Humanitarian Community*, Westview Press, Boulder, CO.

Molander, J. (1995) 'Getting Together to Ban the Use of Blinding Laser Weapons', *Herald Tribune*, 18 December.

Morris, C., Morris, J. and Baines, T. (1995) 'Weapons of Mass Protection: Nonlethality, Information Warfare, and Airpower in the Age of Chaos', *Airpower Journal*, Spring, pp. 15–29.

Morris, C. and Morris, J. (1995) 'End Battle Over Nonlethals', *Defense News*, 13–19 November, p. 40.

Morris, J and Morris, C. (1994) *Nonlethality: A Global Strategy*. Box 312, West Hyannisport, MA 02672.

Morris, J., Krivorotov, V. and Morris, C. (1993) *The Age of Chaos: Threat and Solution Beyond Containment: A Framework for Nonlethal Peacemaking and Peacekeeping*, Box 312, West Hyannisport, MA 02672.

Morris, S. (1957) *The Arm of the Law: United Nations and the Use of Force*, Peace News Pamphlet, Peace News, London.

Morrison, D. (1995) 'More-Than-Lethal Weapons', *National Journal*, 22 July.

Munro, N and Opall, B. (1992) 'Military Studies Unusual Arsenal', *Defense News*, 19–20 October, p. 3.

Narayanamurti, V. and Arvizu, D. (1991), 'Using Sandia Technologies to Improve National Competitiveness', *AT&T Technical Journal*, Vol. 70, No. 6, pp. 2–9.

National Defense Authorization Act For Fiscal Year 1996 (1995) Calendar No. 145 *Section 218: Nonlethal Weapons Programme*, US Government Printing Office, Washington DC, p. 108.

New Scientist (1973) 'Anti-crowd Weapon Works by Causing Fits', 29 March, p. 726.

O'Connell, E. and Dillapain, J. (1994) 'Nonlethal Concepts: Implication for Air Force Intelligence', *Airpower Journal*, Vol. 8, Part 4, pp. 26–33.

Office of Science and Technology (1995) *Technology Foresight – Defense and Aerospace*.

Opall, B. (1992) 'Pentagon Forges Strategy on Non-Lethal Warfare', *Defence Weekly*, Vol. 7, No. 7, 17 February.

Opall, B. (1994) 'DoD to Boost Nonlethal Options', *Defense News*, 28 March–3 April, p. 46.

OTA (Office of Technology Assessment) (1993), *Defense Conversion: Redirecting Defense R&D*, OTA, Washington DC.

Pallister, D. (1994) 'When Food Relief Comes Out of the Barrel of a Gun', *Guardian*, 7 May.

Pallister, D. (1995a) 'Minister Admits "Torture" Baton Export Licence', *Guardian*, 12 August.

Pallister, D. (1995b) ' BAe Man in Arms Sales Team', *Guardian*, 6 September.

Pallister, D. (1996) 'British Firms Still Offering "Shock Batons" Abroad', *Guardian*, 13 March.

Panvel, B. (1994) *Benign Intervention: A Three-Stage Process Initiated by an Impartial*

UN Non-lethal Force Intervening to Halt Armed Conflict, MA dissertation, Department of Peace Studies, University of Bradford.

Parent, C. (1995) 'Support For Non-lethal Technologies Increasing Among NATO Countries', *Inside the Pentagon*, 27 July, p. 4.

Parke, T.R.J. et al. (1992) 'Response to the Kurdish Refugee Crisis by the Edinburgh MEDIC 1 Team', *British Medical Journal*, Vol. 304, 14 March, pp. 695–7.

Pemberton, M. (1994) 'Robocop IV: Dual-use Comes to Police Work', *New Economy*, Summer, p. 11.

Pengelley, R. (1994) 'Wanted: A Watch on Non-lethal Weapons', *International Defense Review*, April, p. 1.

Peters, A. (1996) 'Blinding Laser Weapons'. *Medicine, Conflict and Survival*, Vol. 12, No. 2, April–June, pp. 107–13.

Picatinny Arsenal, NJ (1992) 'ARDEC Exploring Less-than-lethal Munitions; To Give Army Greater Flexibility in Future Conflicts' news release, 9 October.

Pohling-Brown, P. (1994) 'Technologies for America's New Course', *International Defense Review*, October, pp. 33–8.

Prokosch, E. (1995) *The Technology of Killing: A Military and Political History of Anti-personnel Weapons*, Zed Books, London.

Ramsbotham, O. and Woodhouse, T. (1996) *Humanitarian Intervention in Contemporary Conflict*, Polity Press, Cambridge.

Reiss, E. (1992) *The Strategic Defense Initiative*, Cambridge University Press, Cambridge.

Renner, M. (1992), *Economic Adjustments after the Cold War: Strategies for Conversion*, UNIDIR, Geneva.

Riddell-Dixon, E. (1995) 'Social Movements and the United Nations', *International Social Science Journal*, June, pp. 289–303.

Roberts, A. and Guelff, R. (1989) *Documents on the Laws of War*, 2nd edn, Clarendon Press, Oxford.

Robinson, J. (1996) 'DoD Reprogrammes $5.2 Million in FY '96 for Non-lethal Weapons', *Defense Daily*, March 27.

Rodwell, R. (1973) 'How Dangerous is the Army's Squawk Box?', *New Scientist*, 27 September, p. 730.

Rogers, P. (1995) ' New US Weapon Destroys Electrics but Not People', *New Statesman and Society*, 9 June.

Roland-Price, A. (1995) *Non-lethal Weapons – A Synopsis*, DGD&D Position Paper, unpublished.

Roos, J. (1993) 'The Perils of Peacekeeping: Tallying the Costs in Blood, Coin, Prestige, and Readiness', *Armed Forces Journal International*, December, pp. 13–17.

Rose, S. (1968) *Chemical and Biological Warfare: Its Scope, Implications, and Future Development*, George G. Harrap, London.

Rosenberg, B. (1994) 'Non-lethal' Weapons May Violate Treaties', *Bulletin of the Atomic Scientists*, Vol. 50, No. 5, pp. 44–5.

Rosenhead, J. (1976) 'A New Look at "Less Lethal" Weapons', *New Scientist*,

16 December, p. 672.

Rothstein, L. (1994) 'The "Soft-kill" Solution', *Bulletin of the Atomic Scientists*, Vol. 50, No. 2, pp. 4–6.

Rufin, J.-C. (1993) 'The Paradoxes of Armed Protection', in Jean, F. (ed.), *Life, Death and Aid: The Médecins Sans Frontières Report on World Crisis Intervention*, Routledge, London.

Russell, D. 'Non-Lethal Weapons', *Prevailing Winds*, Premiere Issue, Santa Barbara, CA.

Sapolsky, H. (1993) *Non-lethal Warfare Technologies: Opprtunities and Problems*, Defense and Arms Control Studies programme, Massachusetts Institute of Technology, June.

Sapolsky, H. and Shapiro, J. (1996) 'Casualties, Technology, and America's Future Wars', *Parameters*, Summer, pp. 119–27.

Scheffer, D. and Gardner, R. (1992) *Three Views on the Issue of Humanitarian Intervention*, United States Institute for Peace, Washington DC.

Schmitt, E. (1995) 'Somalia Marines to Test Foam Gun', *Guardian*, 16 February.

Schnabel, J. (1995) 'Tinker, Tailor, Soldier, Psi', *Independent on Sunday*, 27 August, pp. 10, 11, 13.

Scott, W.S. (1995) 'Panel's Report Backs Nonlethal Weapons', *Aviation Week and Space Technology*, Vol. 143, 16 October.

Security Planning Corporation. (1972) *Nonlethal Weapons for Law Enforcement: Research Needs and Priorities*, Security Planning Corporation, Washington DC, March.

Sederberg, P. (1995) 'Conciliation as Counter-Terrorist Strategy', *Journal of Peace Research*, Vol. 32, No. 3, pp. 295–312.

Sharp, T., Ray, Y. and Malone, J. (1994) 'US Military Forces and Emergency International Humanitarian Assistance', *Journal of the American Medical Association*, Vol. 272, No. 5, August, pp. 386–90.

Shukman, D. (1995) *The Sorcerer's Challenge: Fears and Hopes for the Weapons of the Next Millennium.* Hodder & Stoughton, London, Chapter 8: 'Bloodless Victory'.

Singer, M. and Wildavsky, A. (1993) *The Real World Order: Zones of Peace and Zones of Turmoil,* Chatham House, USA.

SIPRI (1976) *The Law of War and Dubious Weapons*, SIPRI, Stockholm.

SIPRI (1978) *Anti-personnel Weapons*, Taylor & Francis, London. Chapter 8: 'Electric, Acoustic and Electromagnetic-wave Weapons'.

SIPRI (1981) *World Armaments and Disarmament*, Oxford University Press, Oxford. Chapter 15: 'The Prohibition of Inhumane and Indiscriminate Weapons'.

Speser, P. (1993) 'Public Debate Needed on Laser Weapons', *Laser Focus World*, September, p. 17.

Stanton, M. (1996) 'What Price Sticky Foam?', *Proceedings*, January, pp. 58–60.

Starr, B. (1993) 'Nonlethal Weapon Puzzle for US Army', *International Defense Review*, April, pp. 319–20.

Starr, B. (1994) 'US Group to Assess Military "Revolution"', *Jane's Defence Weekly*, 16 April, p. 20.

Starr, B. (1996) 'USMC Proposed to Lead in Non-lethal Weapons', *Jane's Defence Weekly*, 27 March, p. 6.

Stiefel, M. (1993) 'Humanitarian Assistance and North–South Relations: Interference or Co-operation', *South Letter*, Autumn, pp. 16–18.

Sweetman, S. (1987) *Report on the Attorney General's Conference on Less Than Lethal Weapons*, US Department of Justice/National Institute of Justice, Office of Communication and Research Utilization, March.

Swett, C. (1994) *Future Low-intensity Conflict Environment. Office of the Assistant Secretary of Defense for Special Operations Low-Intensity Conflict, Policy Planning Directorate*, Briefing given at the Sixth Annual SO/LIC-CD Symposium and Exhibition, 'Operations Other Than War: Challenges and Requirements', 14–16 December 1994, Washington DC.

Swinnerton, R. (1993) *The Preparation and Management of Australian Contingents in UN Peacekeeping Operations*, Working Paper No. 275, Strategic and Defence Studies Centre, Australian National University, Canberra, July.

Taylor, S.T. (1995) 'Beating Swords into Police Wares', *Technology Transfer Business*, Winter, pp. 31–5.

Tharoor, S. (1995) 'United Nations Peacekeeping in Europe', *Survival*, Vol. 37, No. 2, pp. 121–34.

Thein, B.K., Shank, E.B. and Wargovitch, M.I. (1974) *Analysis of a 'Bean Bag Type' Projectile as a Less Lethal Weapon*, US Army Land Warfare Laboratory, Aberdeen Proving Ground, Maryland.

Tillman, A. (1994) 'Weapons for the 21st Century Soldier', *International Defense Review*, Vol. 27, No. 1, January, pp. 34–8.

Toffler, A and Toffler, H. (1993) *War and Anti-War: Survival at the Dawn of the 21st Century*, Little, Brown, Boston, MA. Chapter 15: 'War Without Blood?'

Travis, A. (1995) 'Police on Beat to Test CS Gas for Protection', *Guardian*, 14 April.

Tritten, J. (1995) 'Naval Perspectives on Military Doctrine', *Naval War College Review*, Vol. XLVIII, Spring, pp. 22–38.

UNHCR (1993) *The State of the World's Refugees: The Challenge of Protection*, Penguin Books, London.

United Nations Association (1965) *What Kind of Peace Force?*, UNA, London, April.

United States Senate – Committee on Armed Services (1995), *National Defense Authorization Act for Fiscal Year 1996*, Washington DC.

Urquhart, B. (1991) 'How the UN Could Break Up Civil Wars', *European*, 31 December.

Van Creveld, M. (1991) *On Future War*, Brassey's, London.

Victorian, A. (1993), 'Non-lethality: John B. Alexander, the Pentagon's Penguin', *Lobster*, June.

Victorian, A. (1994) 'The Department of Energy's Guinea Pigs: A Preliminary Report', *Lobster*, No. 27, pp. 13–15.

Walker, P. (1992) 'Foreign Military Resources for Disaster Relief: An NGO Perspective', *Disasters*, Vol. 16, No. 2, pp. 152–9.

Waskow, A. (1967) *Toward A Peacekeepers Academy: A Proposal for a First Step Toward a United Nations Transnational Peacekeeping Force*, Dr W.J. Junk Publishers, The Hague.

Weber, T. (1995) 'The Evolution of Plans for an International Military Force for Peace', *Peace Research*, Vol. 27, No. 1, pp. 31–45.

Weiner, T. (1990) *The Pentagon's Black Budget*, Warner Books, New York.

Weinschenk, A. (1993a) 'Boosters are Again Pushing for "Office of Non-Lethality"', *Defense Week*, 16 February.

Weinschenk, A. (1993b) 'Non-lethal Weapons Group Set to Form in March', *Defense Week*, 24 February, p. 1.

Weiss, T. (1993) 'New Challenges for UN Military Operations: Implementing an Agenda for Peace', *Washington Quarterly*, Winter.

Weiss, T., Forsythe, D. and Coate, R. (1994) *The United Nations and Changing World Politics*, Westview Press, Boulder, CO.

Weiss, T. and Weissman, H. (1990) 'Delivering Humanitarian Assistance in African Armed Conflicts: A Critical Commentary', in Weiss, T. (ed.) *Humanitarian Emergencies and Military Help in Africa*, Macmillan, London.

Wright, J. (1994) 'Shoot Not to Kill', *Guardian*, 19 May.

Young, O. (1995) 'System and Society in World Affairs: Implications for International Organizations, *International Social Science Journal*, June, pp. 197–212.

Younge, G. (1996) 'Police Shun Calls to Ditch CS Spray after Man Dies', *Guardian*, 18 March.

Zaloga, S. (1990) 'Soviets Close to Deploying Battlefield Beam Weapons'. *Armed Forces Journal International*, May.

Zuckerman, S. (1980) 'The Deterrent Illusion', *The Times*, 21 January.

Index

Of related interest from ZED BOOKS

THE TECHNOLOGY OF KILLING
A Military and Political History of
Anti-personnel Weapons
Eric Prokosch

'For decades, the nuclear arms race diverted attention from the immense numbers of civilian casualties caused by indiscriminate antipersonnel weapons. This book describes in chilling detail why these "conventional" weapons have been aptly called "weapons of mass destruction in slow motion".'

Patrick Leahy, United States Senator

'This admirably documented study will bring home to all military men and students of war the appalling long-term damage wrought by the smallest and most commonplace of weapons.'

General Sir Hugh Beach, Council for Arms Control, London

'Thoroughly researched and authoritative, Eric Prokosch's book starkly brings into question what is "conventional" about a class of weapons which have brought death and destruction to so many millions. A brilliant, informative, and desperately needed study.'

Dr John E. Fine, former Executive Director, Physicians for Human Rights

'A ground-breaking book which will alert those campaigning against land mines to the dangers of a host of other anti-personnel weapons.'

Robert O. Muller, Vietnam Veterans of America Foundation

'Its treatment of Vietnam discloses some of the most savage tactics used there by the US military.'

George T. McKahin, Professor of International Relations Emeritus, Cornell University

Vietnam, Afghanistan, Cambodia, Somalia.... More soldiers and civilians have died from land mines and other 'conventional' anti-personnel weapons than from any other type of modern armament. Yet outside defence circles little is known about them. This book is the unique story of the development and widespread proliferation of antipersonnel weapons since World War II. As the author persuasively argues, there is no hope of mitigating the sufferings of war so long as the world refuses to face the moral and practical problems posed by these weapons.

ISBN 1 85649 357 1 (Hb) £39.95/$55.00
ISBN 1 85649 358 X (Pb) £12.95/$19.95

If you would like to order this book and/or obtain copies of Zed catalogues please write to Zed Books, 7 Cynthia Street, London N1 9JF, UK, enclosing a cheque as appropriate. Alternatively, ring 0171-837 4014 or fax 0171-833 3960 for credit-card sales. Please add £1.50 per copy for postage and packing in the UK and £2.00/$3.50 per copy to all other addresses.